**THE DARWEN COUNTY
HISTORY SERIES**

A History of
BRISTOL AND
GLOUCESTERSHIRE

St Mary Redcliffe church, Bristol, by night.

THE DARWEN COUNTY HISTORY SERIES

A History of
BRISTOL AND GLOUCESTERSHIRE

Brian S. Smith
and Elizabeth Ralph

Phillimore

First published 1972
Second edition 1982
Third edition 1996

Published by
PHILLIMORE & CO. LTD.
Shopwyke Manor Barn, Chichester, West Sussex

ISBN 0 85033 993 6

Printed and bound in Great Britain by
BUTLER & TANNER LTD.
Frome and London

Contents

Acknowledgements

The line drawings are by the late Miss E.B. Middleton, whose obituary appeared in the *Gloucester Citizen*, 16 February 1987.

We are grateful to the following for their permission to publish photographic illustrations: Russell Adams, 153; W.R. Bawden, Eagle Photos, Cheltenham, 23, 29, 61; Bristol City Museum and Art Gallery, 48, 54, 71, 96-8, 101, 102, 132, 140; Bristol City Public Relations Office, plates II, V, frontispiece, 35, 142; Bristol Port Company, plate XIV; Bristol Record Office, IV, 126; Bristol University, XI (Martin Haswell), 104 (reproduced by kind permission of the Warden); British Aerospace and British Airways, 133; Corinium Museum, Cirencester, 14; Cheltenham Museum and Art Gallery, 82, 112; Pat Cox, 26, 31, 52, 62, 87, 115, 116; Dean Heritage Museum Trust, 80, 81; Paul Felix, plates I, VI, VII; S.R. Gardiner, 129; Gloucestershire Collection, Gloucester City Library, 59, 144; Gloucester City Museum and Art Gallery, dustjacket and plate XIII; Gloucestershire Record Office, plate X, 46, 88, 122, 123, 145; Iris Hardwick, 130; John Jurica, 105; David Lambert, plate IX; © Crown copyright MOD. Reproduced with the permission of the Controller of HMSO, 7; RCHME, © Crown copyright, 30; Peter Turner, 2, 4, 50, 119; Woodchester Parochial Church Council, 15.

The remainder of the plates and photographs are by Brian Smith, particular thanks being owed to Gloucestershire Record Office (110, 148), Mr. G. Simmons (79) and Renishaw plc (94).

List of Illustrations

Frontispiece: St Mary Redcliffe church, Bristol, by night

List of Colour Illustrations

Preface

There are many excellent books about the history of Gloucestershire and others about Bristol. But in writing this one we have had in mind the reader who wants a concise and comprehensive history of both the city and county together. No history of Gloucestershire is complete without the inclusion of Bristol, a city which has strongly influenced the development of its neighbourhood and in turn drawn upon the material and human resources of Gloucestershire.

Administrative boundaries of parish, county and nation have a historical origin and come to create a historical unity among their inhabitants. For a thousand years the long arm of the county sheriff or magistrate sitting in Gloucester reached to the banks of the river Avon at Bristol. For the last six centuries the city of Bristol was also a county. Then, for a few years from 1974 to 1996 a new county of Avon existed briefly, formed from the cities of Bristol and Bath and the adjacent parts of Gloucestershire and Somerset, before the local government map was again redrawn to revert to a more recognisable historical pattern. Such changes may disturb but cannot remove the older administrative, social and economic links which have bound the whole of Gloucestershire and the city of Bristol over many centuries. This book sets out to describe how these links were forged.

A book of this length cannot, of course, pretend to be more than an introduction to a long, colourful, and sometimes complex story. Nevertheless, we wished to refer to all the chief aspects of our local history—hence the large number of chapters for so short a book—and at the same time share some of the unpublished evidence and anecdotes from the records which we, as archivists, have had the privilege to care for. The many unavoidable omissions of facts and details are made good partly by the Bibliography (where books are suggested for further reading) and partly by the Maps. The latter are an important and integral part of the book, and we hope that they will be of general and lasting benefit to Gloucestershire and Bristol historians. The task of portraying so much evidence by way of maps in such a clear and attractive manner has been the achievement of our cartographer, the late Miss E.B. Middleton of Gloucester, to whom we owe a special debt. She also drew for us all the marginal line drawings, the first of the Darwen County Histories to be so illustrated.

It is a pleasant duty to thank those who have helped us, especially our colleagues in the Bristol Record Office and Gloucestershire Record Office. Dr. P.J. Fowler and Dr. C.E. Hart have been generous in improving our chapters on their special subjects of prehistoric and Roman Gloucestershire and the Forest of Dean respectively. We had indispensable help relating to a host of problems from the staff of the Bristol City Museum and Art Gallery, the Gloucester City Library, and the Gloucestershire County Library. On more specific matters concerning their own fields, and in particular with assistance in the preparation of the maps, we wish to thank the planning departments of Bristol Corporation and Gloucestershire and Avon County Councils; the Engineering Departments of British Rail at Gloucester and Bristol; Bristol Port Authority; and the Gloucestershire Branch of the National Farmers' Union. As is so often the custom, proof-reading and indexing have been added to the other burdens that the wife of an author has to bear. Finally, the experience and advice of our publisher has made the creation and production of the *History* a real pleasure.

1

The Landscape

Gloucestershire lies across the mouth of the Severn estuary between the Midlands and the West Country. It is a rural county with only one large urban area formed by the neighbouring towns of Gloucester and Cheltenham. The great city of Bristol originally lay within its southern boundary. But the commercial importance of Bristol was such that as long ago as 1373 it was separated from Gloucestershire, and with its immediate Somerset suburbs created a county in its own right.

The popular notion among strangers that the Cotswolds are typical of the county's landscape is far from true. The scenery is in fact very varied. England's two longest rivers are navigable within the county boundary, and yet on the other hand the Cotswolds are the highest ground in the Lowland Zone of Britain. In a leisurely day's journey a motorist can drive from unmistakeable Thames Valley meadowland over the Cotswold Hills and into the Vale of the Severn. The north of the Vale is characteristic of much of Midland England, while the villages in the south of the Vale resemble those of Somerset. Continuing westwards across the Severn the traveller enters one of the last surviving great forests of the country amid hills which beckon to the higher mountains beyond the Welsh Marches. This variety of landscape has influenced the

1 *Four Shires Stone, Moreton-in-Marsh.*

2 *Cotswold, Vale and Forest from between Dursley and Wotton-under-Edge. The Tyndale Monument stands on the scarp, with Nibley Green, Berkeley power station and castle near the Severn, and Lydney on the far bank.*

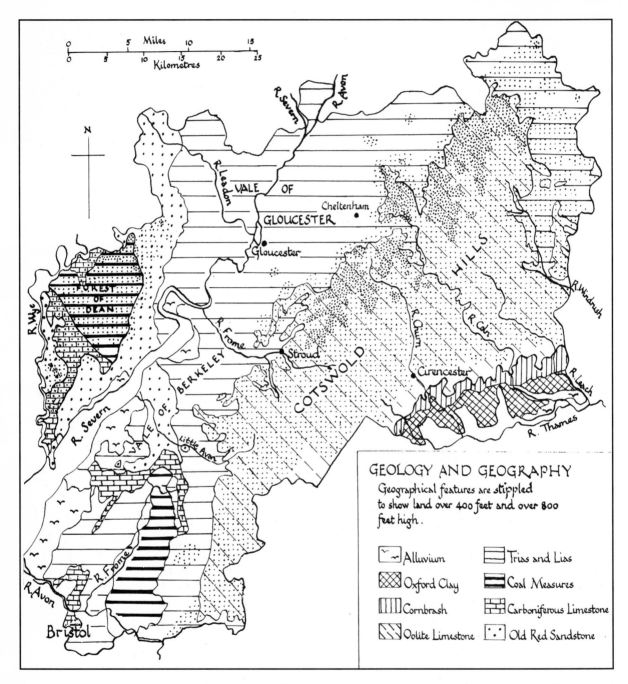

3 *Geology and geo-graphy.*

sites and types of villages and houses, and the choice of livelihood of
their inhabitants, and is caused by the nature of the underlying rocks and
soil.

The Cotswolds are made up of two kinds of oolitic limestone which
are so tilted that they rise gently from the Thames Valley clay and fall

abruptly 400 to 600 feet all along the escarpment from near Chipping Campden to Bath. In colour the stone is almost white in the south, turning a deep golden brown in the north where it is tinted with ironstone. Where the two layers of limestone meet is a thin joint of fuller's earth of soft, soapy texture, ideal for the washing and fulling (or felting) of wool in the manufacture of cloth. It is also the point where springs force through the limestone so that many early dwellings are found on it. The stone is good for building but in fact was not univer-

4 *Huntsman's Quarry, one of the few surviving Cotswold stone quarries.*

sally used until Tudor times because there was also plenty of woodland, and timber is easier to build with. Some ancient Cotswold woods survive, like the Buckholt (Saxon, 'beech wood') at Cranham and the box wood after which Boxwell was named at least nine hundred years ago. The steep edge is split by fast westward-flowing streams so good for driving watermills. Above the valleys the flattish wolds formerly made better sheep pasture than tillage, but towards the Thames Valley is a strip of cornbrash suitable for rich arable farming.

Much of the Vale east of the River Severn is formed of a stiff clay which makes a heavy waterlogged soil best suited for dairy farming. South of Berkeley the underlying rock is more varied; the reddish Forest of Dean sandstone reappears near Thornbury and Berkeley, while carboniferous limestone is quarried near Chipping Sodbury and a coalfield, no longer worked, stretches north from Bitton to Cromhall.

The Severn itself is an important feature of the Vale, bisecting the countryside from Tewkesbury to Bristol. It was formed in its present course when the melting waters of the last Ice Age burst through the cliffs at Ironbridge in Shropshire and thereafter flowed southwards instead of north to the Dee. In its broad estuary the tide has one of the largest falls in the world, and as it races up the funnel of the river mouth it forms a head, known as the bore, which in spring sometimes advances as a wall of water up to two metres high as far as the weirs at Gloucester. The river in flood can cause immense havoc, as in 1607 and 1947, and 1770 when the highest known flood of over 11 metres was recorded at Gloucester.

The Severn has always been a great trade route, and in their season salmon, lampreys and elvers have provided the riverside villagers with a means of livelihood. The river is not easy to navigate for its channel is shallow and it possesses a well-earned reputation for changing its course and shifting its shoals and sandbanks. In 1172 the river washed away an

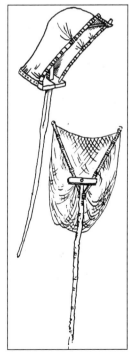

5 *Elver net and salmon lave net.*

6 *Camp Mill, Soudley, now the Dean Heritage Centre, stands on the site of a 17th-century iron–works.*

extensive piece of land at Slimbridge and piled it up on the Awre side. Then about 1570 it changed course again, and eroded the Awre bank. John Smith of Nibley recalled how the Slimbridge New Grounds, now the site of the Severn Wildfowl Trust, had 'byn cast togeather and left by the river of Severne, ... it being then remembred (even by my selfe) when a great part of those grounds were the body and main part of the channell it selfe and the deepest part thereof'.

West of the Severn successive bands of clay and sandstone form rolling wooded hills where orchards flourish, and beyond these the coal measures of the Forest of Dean overlie iron ore beds. The Forest is still heavily wooded, shaped like a horseshoe with the higher ground at the edge, dropping on the extreme western boundary in sheer limestone cliffs 75 metres to the River Wye. The inaccessibility of the Forest, where the men have been pioneers in mining, encroaching and settling in the royal woods, has given its inhabitants an independent character, which may account for the commercial success of some Foresters who have become leading citizens of Bristol.

7 *Belas Knap, a Neolithic long barrow on Cleeve Hill above Winchcombe.*

2

Prehistoric and Roman Gloucestershire

This chapter must begin with a warning. Very recent archaeological discoveries and scientific techniques are causing a general revision of the chronology and patterns of prehistory, although it will be years before all the implications are worked out and a new framework proved and accepted. It is being found that many prehistoric events took place over a much longer span of time and more peacefully than was formerly believed. Therefore hitherto accepted theories about the distribution and occupation of sites and the external influences on prehistoric peoples can no longer be confidently asserted. The sequence of events within Britain may not be greatly different from the familiar pattern of Neolithic Age, Bronze Age and Iron Age—terms which are retained here—but the reader must remember that changes took place very slowly and the influence of new cultures from the Continent was not sudden, that some sites were occupied for a very long period, and that over the four thousand years before the Roman occupation different types of culture and different groups of inhabitants merged one with another, and overlapped each other in both time and space.

8 *Birdlip mirror.*

Primitive men have left their traces in the valleys of the Thames and Bristol Avon and at Barnwood near Gloucester, but the first permanent settlement of the area which is now Gloucestershire did not occur until after the last Ice Age, some 10,000 years ago when Britain had become an island. Some discoveries of Mesolithic flints have been made mostly on the Cotswolds, but the earliest extensive prehistoric relics in the county date from the Neolithic period, beginning about 4000 B.C. All over the Cotswolds are the great communal stone tombs called long barrows. The best-known examples of the two main types are Hetty Pegler's Tump near Uley, where the central burial chamber can be entered, and Belas Knap on Cleeve Hill, which is almost 60 metres long and contained some 38 skeletons. The Neolithic people who built the long barrows were not only hunters and herdsmen, but also the first farmers with tools capable of clearing the wildwood and cultivating lowland sites, although the distribution of the long barrows suggests that they preferred the lighter soils of the Cotswold hills and valleys to the Vale. There they constructed the earliest causewayed hill-camps like Crickley. For heavy work they imported polished stone axe-heads from North Wales, the Lake District and even overseas, while for hunting and perhaps for warfare they armed themselves with leaf shaped arrowheads of flint from the Marlborough Downs.

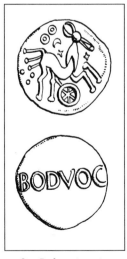

9 *Dobunnic coin.*

During the warmer centuries of the Bronze Age from about 2000 to 700 B.C. Gloucestershire remained only thinly populated compared with the Wessex downs. The biggest concentration of surviving Bronze-Age burial mounds, or round barrows for single burials, is between Stow and Cheltenham though there were also many in the upper Thames valley. These people of the Bronze Age were notable traders, who established a strong link between Ireland and southern England, where most of them lived on the Wiltshire and Dorset downs. Their route lay by way of the Bristol Avon and Severn estuary; the great stones from the Prescelly Hills in Pembrokeshire, used in the construction of Stonehenge, may have been transported this way. The earth bank of a more modest henge can be traced at Condicote near Stow.

Iron-Age influence and immigration spread about 550 B.C. both from the mouth of the Severn and from the eastern Cotswolds. The earliest simple univallate earthworks like that at Crickley date from the transitional period of Bronze-Age and Iron-Age cultures between about 700 and 100 B.C. In succeeding centuries different Iron-Age farming peoples become easier to identify from the types of pottery that they manufactured and the earthworks that they constructed. The whole length of the Cotswold escarpment is crowned with hill forts and, although some of these earthworks were perhaps originally built not as military defences but as agricultural stockades, they must have been local centres of power and trade in the last centuries B.C. The great multivallate forts with two or more ramparts date from this period, massive and complex works like the hilltop sites at Painswick, Uley Bury and Sodbury. At the defended settlement at Salmonsbury, near Bourton-on-the-Water, a 60-acre site which had been occupied for several centuries, many iron currency bars were discovered in 1860. These were probably manufactured in the Forest of Dean, where at Lydney there was another hill fort of the same group, and they have also been found at Uley Bury and North Cerney and in some numbers on Meon Hill (Warwicks.) and at Malvern (Worcs.). In the last century or so before the Roman occupation there was further migration to the Vale and the country immediately to the west of the Severn by people who had close trading connections with the western coasts of Roman Europe, and their arrival was perhaps accompanied by warfare.

By the late first century B.C. a tribe called the Dobunni occupied Gloucestershire east of the Severn Vale, and much of modern Oxfordshire. The earthworks at Minchinhampton may have been a tribal capital. About A.D. 10, under strong influence or perhaps actual conquest by the Catuvellauni of eastern Britain, they built another capital at Bagendon. From about A.D. 25 to 50 the 'town' and its surroundings extended over 200 acres, protected by earthworks. Within these were substantial timber-framed and thatched houses, forges and stock inclosures, indicating an economy that included mixed farming and metalworking. Iron from the Forest of Dean, lead from the Mendips, together with rarer metals from farther afield, tin, copper and gold, were

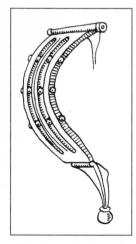

10 *Bagendon brooch.*

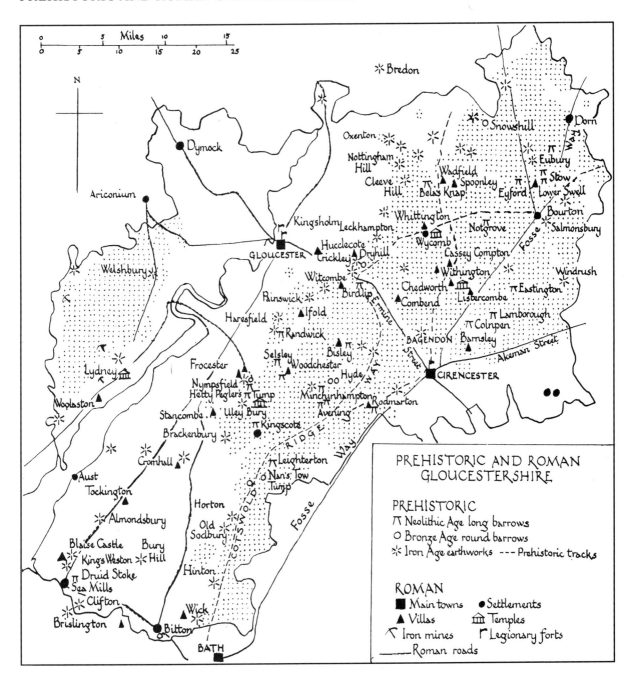

mined to supply the smiths' workshops. Coins, weapons, tools and ornaments, including a distinctive style of brooch peculiar to Bagendon, were manufactured for use at home and for export. In return the Dobunni obtained pottery from Gaul, glass from the Levant, and knowledge of the might of the Roman empire.

11 *Prehistoric and Roman Gloucestershire.*

12 *Rufus Sita.*

Politically they were allied to the Catuvellauni until the Roman invasion of A.D. 43, and the earthworks at Minchinhampton and Bagendon may be compared with those at St Albans and Colchester. The Dobunni then became divided in their loyalties. Bodvoc, king of the northern part of the tribe at Bagendon, was pro-Roman, and about A.D. 47 Roman troops advanced to establish a base for his protection. Through this base at Cirencester, a short distance from the tribal capital, a boundary was drawn by the construction of the Fosse Way from Exeter to Lincoln. The southern Dobunni under the leadership of their chief Corio and Caratacus, the defeated leader of the Catuvellauni, may have continued local resistance. If so, Ostorius Scapula, the Roman general, outflanked them by setting up advance camps at Kingsholm, near Gloucester, and *Abone* at Sea Mills.

The territory between the Fosse Way and the Severn remained a military zone, the Kingsholm camp being abandoned in favour of the neighbouring higher ground at Gloucester, where the first legionary fort was constructed about A.D. 65. The tombstone of one of these first soldiers to be stationed at Gloucester, who came from Bulgaria, commemorates, 'Rufus Sita, a cavalryman of the Sixth Cohort of the Thracians, after forty years of life and twenty two years of military service'. He is shown armed with helmet, shield, heavy sword and spear, riding down and thrusting at a fallen enemy. From *Abone* and Gloucester the Silures of South Wales were conquered in A.D. 74-78; a few years later the legion then stationed at Gloucester was posted forward forty miles to Caerleon.

13 *Blackpool Bridge. The cobbled Roman trackway in the Forest of Dean.*

Bodvoc had apparently moved into the Roman legionary fort at

Cirencester soon after the arrival of the troops, whose presence was no longer necessary after about A.D. 75. Much rebuilding followed, and when about 175 a great earthen town wall was built it enclosed a coffin-shaped area of 96 hectares, five times the size of Gloucester and the second biggest town in Britain; only London was larger. The traveller from London entered the town by a bridge over the moat, and then through a massive 30-metre-wide stone gate, comprising two large archways for wheeled traffic flanked by two pedestrian gates. Watchmen and officials could observe him from the projecting towers of the walls, which were refaced in stone about 225. Inside the walls first-century timber-framed houses mingled with the growing number of stone buildings erected during the third century. The main street from London ran straight to the forum. This great open market place and courtyard spread for over 100 metres, surrounded by shops and administrative buildings, the largest of which was the government offices and law courts, called the basilicum. The prosperity of Cirencester reached its fullest extent in the fourth century when under the emperor Diocletian it became the provincial capital of one of the four governors of Britain. Many buildings were enlarged and the best mosaic pavements date from this period. There was a theatre and outside the town walls an amphi-theatre seating 6,000. The popula-tion was probably 5,000 to 10,000.

14 *Celtic-Roman mother goddesses, Ciren-cester. Three figures in civilian dress holding bas-kets of fruit and loaves, symbolising fertility.*

Gloucester was much smaller. Twenty years after the legion left, the town was created a *colonia* (a privileged self-governing town for retired soldiers, who received grants of neighbouring land attached to the township). Its plan was square, with stone walls and gates, and main streets of colonnaded buildings. South of the modern Cross the site of the forum and basilicum was discovered in 1968-9. There were a few other settlements of a minor urban nature, among which *Abone* at Sea Mills, as a ferry terminal and trading port, and *Ariconium* (Herefords.) with smelting furnaces, were linked with the iron mines in the Forest of Dean. A cobbled packhorse Roman road ran through the heart of the iron mining area where the Roman workings are locally called 'scowles'.

One of these mines is close to the late Roman hilltop temple outside Lydney dedicated to Nodens, a local god perhaps representing the Severn itself. He apparently possessed the power of healing, for the temple has a range of rooms for wealthy patients and worshippers staying at the adja-cent guest house to prepare themselves for entering the sanctuary. This remarkable complex of buildings dates from about 364-7, when the sea-board was already being seriously troubled by pirate raids. A reminder of the presence of a fleet in the Bristol Channel based at Cardiff is seen in the gift of a new mosaic floor at the temple of Nodens by the commander of the supply depot of the fleet.

Facing it directly across the Severn from the Cotswold edge at Uley is an equally remarkable Romano-Celtic temple dedicated to Mercury. It stood on a site hallowed from Neolithic times and close to the Iron-Age fort of Uley Bury. At the height of its fame in the fourth century the stone-built temple with its complex of shops and other buildings was extensively patronised by wealthy pilgrims and worshippers who show-ered upon the god their votive offerings of statuettes, inscribed lead tablets and coins. Later, in the fifth to sixth centuries a small Christian church stood there.

In the countryside from at least early in the second century small timber-framed villas were built. The most favoured sites for these coun-try estates seem to have been in the Cotswold valleys or under the escarpment. In the late third and fourth centuries the villas were rebuilt

15 *Woodchester. The great Roman villa with the largest mosaic floors north of the Alps lies beneath the church and churchyard.*

in stone, and new mosaic pavements were laid at Hucclecote as late as 395. The most spectacular of all these floors and the largest in northern Europe shows the legend of Orpheus taming the wild beasts in the great house at Woodchester. The Woodchester villa was built about 350-70 around two courtyards but another common arrangement was a long house with a corridor down one side as at Chedworth.

The villas, of which about fifty are known in northern and mid-Gloucestershire, were the centres of Romanised country estates. Beyond them were several hundred humbler Romano-British villages and farms, so that the distribution maps of villa sites do not give a true indication of the population in the countryside. Possibly the rural population in the fourth century was as great as in 1086, and very many Romano-British settlements still lie hidden, especially in the Thames valley. Some thirty previously unknown ones were discovered by archaeologists in 1969-70 along the M5 motorway route in Gloucestershire, a strip of land a mere 50 yards wide.

The isolated villas and settlements were particularly vulnerable to attacks from marauders once the Roman defensive system weakened. In 367 there was a co-ordinated barbarian attack on Britain, and villas near the sea like Kings Weston were probably not inhabited much afterwards. The town walls at both Cirencester and Gloucester were strengthened in the mid-fourth century, and after 400, if not before, many wealthy villa owners sought their security, leaving the country mansions to estate officials and eventually to squatters.

3

Saxon Gloucestershire

After the Roman garrisons were withdrawn in 410 and the final links with the Empire broken in 446, British warlords resisted the penetration of the Saxons for several generations. It was not until about 525 that a band of Saxons, having made their way up the Thames Valley, first settled in Gloucestershire at Fairford. The victory of Ceawlin, the first great king of Wessex, over three petty British kings of Gloucestershire and north Somerset marked a fresh advance in 577. It is recorded in the Anglo-Saxon Chronicle that 'in this year Cuthwine and Ceawlin fought against the Britons and killed three kings, Conmail, Condidan and Farinmail at the place which is called Dyrham; and they captured three of their cities, Gloucester, Cirencester and Bath'. At Gloucester archaeologists have discovered evidence of burning and slaughter, but the victors were not numerous enough to settle more than the southern part of the county, their earliest villages including Kemble, Poulton, Avening and the important river crossing at Arlingham.

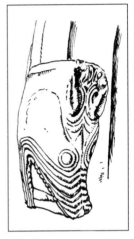

16 *Saxon carving, Deerhurst.*

The north of the county was invaded by Angles, or English, from the Fens who founded villages at Beckford and Ebrington. Their slow colonisation was strengthened by the victory of Penda of Mercia over the West Saxons at Cirencester in 628. He then established a new kingdom dependent on Mercia, with Angles and Saxons combined under rulers drawn from the Northumbrian royal family. This kingdom of the Hwicce comprised all Gloucestershire east of the Severn, most of Worcestershire and west Warwickshire.

Throughout the seventh and eighth centuries the Saxons multiplied, establishing farms and villages. Although they enslaved numbers of Britons, place-names bear witness to the apparently peaceful survival of groups of 'Welshmen', for example at Walham, Walton and Wallsworth, and other names of Welsh origin are found, particularly in west Gloucestershire. By 1066 nearly all the villages in Gloucestershire had been founded, and the land about them cleared and divided, usually into two great open fields where the farmers cultivated unhedged one-acre strips side by side. In some cases where the Roman villa estates had not reverted to a wilderness they brought them back into cultivation, as at Withington and probably Dymock, Woodchester, Barnsley and Frocester, but they showed no interest in repairing the ruined villas or the more substantial buildings in Gloucester and Cirencester.

17 Deerhurst priory church church dates from the earliest days of Christianity in Gloucestershire. The oldest parts of the nave and tower were built before 800, the whole church being enlarged and partly rebuilt in the 10th century.

Both these towns were in such good strategic positions that the Saxons settled in them, but they ignored the crumbling Roman streets and built instead in the open areas just within or outside the city walls. At Cirencester they chose the space in the extreme north of the Roman town, and at Gloucester the riverside quarter outside the west gate. At Cirencester the Roman walls at the other end of the town collapsed and caused flooding at Watermoor. At Gloucester there may have been some administrative continuity but the town was refounded in the early tenth century by Ethelfleda, daughter of king Alfred, and its centre remained deserted and weed-infested until the 13th century.

The Saxons were heathen. In 603 the Hwicce witnessed on their borders, perhaps at Aust, the abortive conciliation between St Augustine and the Welsh bishops. St Augustine had been sent from Rome to convert the Saxons to Christianity, but his difficult negotiations with the British churchmen, cut off from contact with Rome for two centuries, were broken off because according to Bede the Welsh 'preferred their own traditions before all the churches in the world'. The Hwicce were themselves not converted until after Penda's death in 654. Their first bishop was appointed in 679, with his cathedral at Worcester and his diocese stretching over all the tribal area as far as the Bristol Avon. Gloucestershire west of the River Leadon lay in the territory of the Magonsaete, in which was now created the bishopric of Hereford, and this division of Gloucestershire between the dioceses of Worcester and Hereford lasted until the Reformation.

Missionary churches with small communities of priests were established in the larger villages like Bishop's Cleeve, Henbury and Withington. Later, and especially in the 150 years before the Norman Conquest, the wide areas served by the missions were divided into parishes as village lords built churches for their people. Many churches contain some indication of Saxon foundation. One of the earliest is the doorway at Somerford Keynes church, which was probably erected when Malmesbury Abbey acquired the estate in 685. At Deerhurst the surviving monastic church was enlarged at least three times before 800, and contains a fine Saxon font; nearby is the simple chapel built in 1056 by Earl Odda in memory of his brother Alfric.

The Hwicce remained part of Mercia during the peak of its power when Offa made his great ditch along its western boundary between 784 and 796. The most impressive local part of Offa's Dyke is between Tidenham and St Briavels where it crowns the steep cliffs overlooking the River Wye and Wales. A century later, after the Hwicce had been

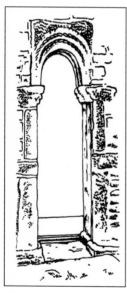

18 Somerford Keynes doorway.

19 *Saxon Gloucestershire.*

absorbed by Wessex, the military importance of Gloucester was again revealed. During the first major Danish invasion Guthrum made Gloucester his base against Alfred from 877 to 879. There was a second wave of Danish invasions in the late tenth century, concluding with Cnut's

20 Winchcombe. The capital of late Saxon Winchcombeshire formerly possessed a Mercian royal palace and a great Benedictine monastery.

succession to the English throne in 1016. It was during the organisation of England to resist these invaders that Gloucester became the capital of one of the new shires created for the military defence of the country between 1000 and 1016.

There were several peculiarities about Gloucestershire. The territory of the Hwicce had included Worcestershire and west Warwickshire, but not the Forest of Dean area. These ancient tribal limits continued to be recognised, for at first Gloucestershire also did not contain the Forest which became part of the shire of Hereford. Furthermore, part of the north of the present county was made a separate shire, centred on Winchcombe, in the heart of Hwiccian territory and then a Mercian royal town containing a palace and an important abbey founded by Cenwulf of Mercia in 798. Both the Forest and Winchcombeshire were incorporated within Gloucestershire by 1066. A third peculiarity was the irregular shape of the boundary due to the ownership of great estates like those of the cathedral of Worcester, all of which were allotted to Worcestershire, even though the result was to create islands of Worcestershire within Gloucestershire. Most of these strange anomalies were abolished in 1844 and 1930-31.

The shires were centred on strategic military sites and major towns which suggests that Bristol was not then of great importance, although it was a thriving seaport. It derived its name from 'Bricgstow', meaning a settlement at the bridge. This was Bristol bridge. The town greatly increased in stature from the early 11th century, yearly enlarging its material substance through trade with Ireland and the neighbouring coasts. Only coins minted in Bristol and a Saxon sculpture depicting the Harrowing of Hell, which was found under the floor of the chapter house of Bristol Cathedral, have survived as evidence of the town's origins.

Gloucester on the other hand was in late Saxon times one of the most important towns in the kingdom. By the time of the Norman Conquest it had a population of up to three thousand, of whom 300 were burgesses. Its trade was largely dependent upon the iron mines of the Forest of Dean, and the presence of a mint indicates its mercantile strength. There were eight churches and two monasteries, and a royal palace at Kingsholm. King Athelstan died at Gloucester in 939 and Ethelred II was crowned there in 1014. Edward the Confessor apparently began the custom of visiting Gloucester to hunt in the Forest, frequently holding royal councils in the city, a practice which was continued by William the Conqueror at Christmas time when he was in England.

4

Gloucestershire in Domesday Book

After the Norman Conquest William I's followers were rewarded with the lands of the dispossessed Saxons lords, and in Gloucestershire William himself seized much of the property that had formerly belonged to King Harold. The king thus became the biggest landowner in the county, owning 109 of the 500 manors, or about a quarter of the land in Gloucestershire. Next was the monastic church of Worcester with 27 manors. Gloucester abbey and the archbishop of Canterbury each had 17 manors, and Winchcombe abbey 13; altogether the Church owned about one quarter of the county. The remainder was by 1086 divided among the Conqueror's supporters, of whom Roger de Lacy with 18 manors in north-west Gloucestershire and the east Cotswolds was the principal. Most of the barons were granted scattered possessions so that they should not build up lordships strong enough to challenge the Crown. In spite of this precaution William I was faced with revolts, one of the most serious of which occurred in 1075 led by Roger, Earl of Hereford, a powerful Gloucestershire landowner.

In order to consolidate the Conquest, royal castles were built at Gloucester, Sharpness and Chepstow. The site chosen at Gloucester was between the town walls and the river, where at least 16 houses were demolished before 1086 to make room, and a further eight in the next few years. Soon after 1100 a new keep was erected, enlarged by the addition of a bailey about 1140, and a new bridge and barbican about 1226. Throughout the 13th and 14th centuries its towers and walls were kept in repair, but after 1460 it was allowed to decay.

William also needed to know more about his newly won kingdom, its landowners and their estates, power and wealth. It was in 1085 that the Anglo-Saxon Chronicle records,

> Then at Midwinter was the King at Gloucester with his Witan, and held there his Court five days ... the King had much thought, and very deep speech with his Witan, about this land; how it was settled or with what manner of men; then he sent over all England, into every Shire, his men, and caused to be made out how many hundred hides were in the Shire, or what land the King himself had, and cattle within the land; or what dues he ought to have in twelve months from the Shire ... . And all the writings were brought to him afterwards.

The 'writings', undertaken and drafted within a year of enormous bureaucratic activity, were put together as Domesday Book.

21 *Domesday Glouces-tershire.*

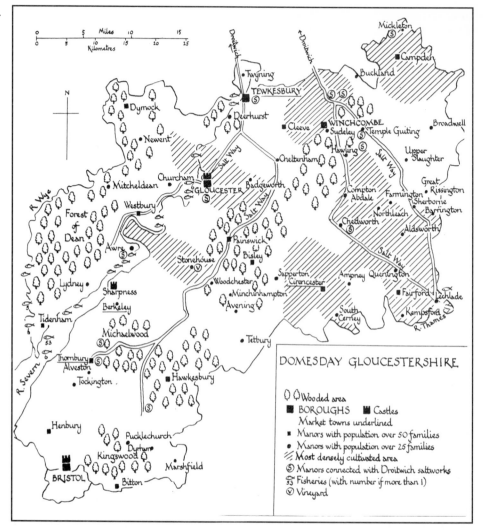

In the county 363 separate settlements are named in Domesday Book, or about the same number of ancient villages that still survive. A few failed, while others are not recorded because they did not then exist, like Coleford, Nailsworth and Stroud, each of which developed in later times. There was a different concentration of population from now. Four boroughs at Bristol, Gloucester, Tewkesbury and Winchcombe are mentioned. Although Domesday has little to say about the town of Bristol, other than that it was part of the royal manor of Barton, it does suggest that Bristol was a seaport of some importance. It paid to the Crown a rent of £84, whilst Gloucester paid £60. In the countryside the most densely populated area was the upper Thames Valley. This was where the Saxons had first settled in the sixth century and the figures reflect their long occupation as well as the rich nature of the farms on the cornbrash. Altogether about 8,000 families are recorded, which suggests that the total population of the county and Bristol was not more than 40.000. The population in 1971, the last census before the radical alteration of the county boundaries with the creation of Avon, was about one million.

Three main classes of countrymen may be identified. About half are described as 'villeins' or villagers—men who mostly farmed about 30 acres (12 hectares) of arable land with pasture rights on the village commons and meadows, and owed the Norman lord of the manor services in return for their farms. At Stoke Orchard in 1314 a villein worked two days a week for most of the year on the home farm of his lord, Gilbert de Clare, Earl of Gloucester, ploughing, harrowing and such other jobs as the farm bailiff might require. During the busiest season of the harvest in August and September he had to work for four days a week, as well as an additional eight days during the harvest itself to carry in the crop. Unless he had a large family his own holding must have suffered, but in turn he might have employed labour from the ranks of the cottagers.

About a quarter of the population of Gloucestershire at the time of Domesday Book were cottagers with small holdings of a few acres, and therefore owing their lords correspondingly smaller services, and another quarter were landless serfs. These men were mostly the descendants of the enslaved inhabitants of Roman Britain. It is remarkable what a large proportion of the population of the west Midlands were serfs; in central and eastern England there were few or none. They obtained a livelihood by hiring themselves out, and if they were fortunate they might earn their freedom, like William Pope of Forthampton, a serf of the abbot of Tewkesbury, in 1454. Alternatively if they were bold enough they might flee the village to a town outside their lord's jurisdiction, as did Walter Bond (his surname recalls that he was a 'bondman' of his lord) who left Newent to become a metalworker in Gloucester in 1396.

The peasant's life was undoubtedly comfortless and hard. The little timber-framed houses were dark and damp. Animals were small and prone to disease, crops low-yielding and weedy, so that endless labour was needed to provide a living. If all landlords were as strict as Gloucester Abbey, labour services and dues were always demanded and rigidly supervised. A visit to market, a journey far afield with the lord's waggons, or a church festival broke the routine of village life. The world was small. Although events like the murder of Edward II at Berkeley in 1327, the execution of the Dukes of Kent and Salisbury in the streets of Cirencester in 1400, and the battle of Tewkesbury in 1471, must have started many rumours and tales, insignificant local happenings were no less memorable.

Nearly twenty years after the event the villagers of Southam near Cheltenham could recall the day in 1357 when Joan Haym was baptised. She was born at one of the larger houses of the village, which is still called Haymes after her family. And what an eventful day it was. Another baby was born in the village on the same day, and a man and a child

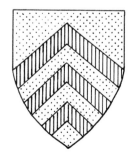

22 *De Clare arms.*

23 *Berkeley Castle. The 14th-century gatehouse flanks the keep, built in 1154-5, where Edward II was murdered.*

died. There was a wedding in one of the well-known village families, and the bishop confirmed a boy from the parish. A freak gale blew down a house, while Joan's baptism generated a whole series of catastrophes. The peasant who went to fetch the water for the font fell into the well. The clergyman who took the service lost his temper with another parishioner, struck him with his stick, and cut his head open, while a third man returning from the church stumbled and broke his leg.

The villages themselves changed little and slowly. Cowley, which was owned by the abbey of Pershore (Worcs.) and leased by the Berkeleys of Coberley, the neighbouring village, may be taken as an example. The church and watermill were possibly the only medieval buildings of stone. Behind the cluster of small houses in the main street, with its preaching cross, were a few gardens and crofts for growing vegetables and protecting the stock in winter. A meadow containing a dovecot, which gave Cowley its name of 'cu-leah' or 'cow-pasture', lay between the village and the River Churn. Above the valley the two great open arable fields, typical of the Cotswolds, stretched for a mile across the wold. They were cultivated and rested in turn. Beyond them and on the steeper hill slopes half the parish consisted of rough pasture, scrubland and dense woods, where the sheep and pigs ran free, and wattle rods could be collected for thatching. During the 13th-century agricultural boom the population increased, and more land was cleared. New hamlets were started at Birdlip and Stockwell about 1200, each with their own open fields divided in strips, like the Cowley ones. This pattern remained relatively undisturbed until the mid-18th century.

Elsewhere the land was made more productive by subdividing the open fields into three, four or more, so that only a third or a quarter lay fallow each year instead of a half. Apart from the forest areas Gloucestershire in 1086 was a prosperous agricultural county, especially the Thames Valley and Vale of the Severn. The number of ploughteams recorded in Domesday Book suggests that about the same amount of land was under the plough then as in 1952, although it is difficult to compare figures precisely because of differing farming practices, particularly the medieval custom of letting some of the ploughland lie fallow each year. So long as there remained enough waste and pasture land, farming changes which did not seriously affect the rights of the villagers were acceptable. The swing from labour services to money rents was more welcome. In the north Cotswolds some landlords requested money

24 *Berkeley arms.*

rents in the 13th century, thus allowing their tenants more flexibility in running their farms. The change became more rapid in the 14th century, especially among absentee lords, like monasteries, who did not wish to work their own distant manors. What was unpopular was the inclosure of open fields where there was a shortage of pasture. In the Vale in the early 13th century Thomas Berkeley 'reduced great quantities of ground into enclosures and severalty, by procuringe many releases of Comon from free holders, wherein hee bestowed much labor ... . For at this tyme, lay all lands in Comon feilds, here one acre or ridge, and there an other, one mans intermixt with an other'. Maurice Berkeley continued the process later in the century, despite the lawsuits of his tenants, who protested at the loss of their common rights.

The fame of Cotswold wool obscures other farming specialities. The medieval Ryeland sheep of Herefordshire and north-west Gloucestershire were even more highly prized than Cotswold flocks, and the county lay astride the drove roads for Welsh cattle. By 1258 Welsh drovers regularly brought their cattle through Newent, where dealers from the Cotswolds attended the market, on their way to Gloucester and over the Welsh Way to the Thames Valley. A vineyard is recorded at Stonehouse in 1086, and forty years later William of Malmesbury commented on the wines of the Severn Valley. In those warmer centuries the abbot of Gloucester had a vineyard at Over and the Earl of Gloucester at Tewkesbury. The bishop of Hereford planted fruit trees at Cheltenham in 1247, and by the late 14th cen-tury cider was made throughout much of west Gloucestershire and the Vale, and even the east Cots-wolds.

25 *Thomas   Lord Berkeley (d.1417).*

It is still possible to trace the ridge and furrow of open fields, par-ticularly when the sun is low or the snow is partly melted, but another feature of medieval farming is easier to find. Watermills for grind-ing corn already existed in 178 vil-lages in 1086, and as mill sites are rarely changed there are many sur-viving (but now disused) mills stand-ing in the very place chosen by the first Saxon miller. By the late 13th century windmills were also being built; their sites are harder to find but the relics of two can be discov-ered at Siddington and Tidenham.

26 *Lower Slaughter water mill, like many mills, probably stands on the site of its Domesday predecessors.*

5

Cotswold Wool

27 *Wool merchants' marks.*

The Cotswolds were one of the great English wool-producing centres throughout the Middle Ages. The Cotswold breed of sheep, of which a few remain, was a relatively large animal with a long fleece. Its wool was coarser and only a quarter of the value of the famous 13th-century 'Leominster ore' fleece of the smaller Herefordshire Ryeland sheep, but Cotswold wool remained in great demand until the improvement of Spanish merino wool in the 18th century.

Long before the Norman Conquest there were sheep farms on the Cotswolds. There are three Shiptons in Gloucestershire, meaning 'sheep farm', as well as less obvious Saxon place-names like Yanworth, which is derived from 'lamb inclosure'. As early as the eighth century Gloucester Abbey had a large flock at Evenlode, and the importance of the Cirencester wool market is indicated in Domesday Book. In the 13th century monastic flocks were greatly enlarged to cope with the export demands of Netherland and Italian cloth manufacturers. By 1306 Gloucester Abbey had over 10,000 sheep producing 46 sacks (each of 356 lbs or a little over 160 kilos) of wool that year, and the Tewkesbury Abbey flock at Stanway was so large in 1340 that the abbey claimed a thousand sheep had been stolen.

Such large flocks required special management. At Sherborne in the 14th century the tenants of the abbot of Winchcombe were obliged to work for 15 days washing and shearing the abbey's sheep, but a hundred years later the work was even better organised. Sherborne became the shearing station for all the abbey's flocks, and in 1485 drovers brought in 2,900 sheep. Quarters were provided for the shearers, and the abbot rode up from Winchcombe to supervise the weighing in a special room, buying up his tenants' wool for resale. A few miles away there was a similar scene at Barrington where the prior of Lanthony near Gloucester watched over the shearing of his flock of 2,000 sheep.

By then large flocks were also owned by the lay landowners like the Berkeleys, and even the peasants kept sheep on the wide village downs. All this was achieved, however, without the extensive destruction of villages that caused so much distress in the east Midlands. There are few deserted medieval village sites in Gloucestershire, because the villages were already widely spaced with generous pastures and it was only some smaller upland hamlets like Roel, Harford and Pinnock which became

1 *Tewkesbury Abbey from the flood meadows. The Benedictine abbey was consecrated in 1121 and bought by the town at the Dissolution.*

II *Bristol Cathedral from College Green, showing the addition of the nave and western towers.*

III *Gloucester Cathedral's tower, completed in 1457, rises above the 13th-century abbey gateway. In the foreground is the monument to Bishop John Hooper on the site where he was burnt at the stake in 1554 as a Protestant heretic.*

decayed. As at Beverstone after its purchase by Thomas Lord Berkeley in 1330, landowners enlarged their flocks by consolidating their scattered lands and converting them to pasture, without depopulating the villages.

The peak period for the export of wool was the mid-14th century when about 30,000 sacks a year left the country. This was when some of the greatest Cotswold wool merchants made their riches, and spent them. In 1401 William Grevel of Chipping Campden died, his memorial brass proclaiming him to have been 'the flower of the wool merchants of all England'. His fine home in Campden is one of the earliest Cotswold stone houses, as befits a wealthy merchant, and in his will he gave generously for the rebuilding of the parish church. At Northleach are memorial brasses to some of the many merchants who rebuilt and enriched that parish church in the 15th century, notably the Fortey family, William Bicknell and John Taylor with his 15 children.

The activities of one of these Northleach woolmen, William Midwinter, are revealed in the correspondence of the Cely family. The latter were London merchants exporting wool to the Low Countries. They travelled each year throughout the north Cotswolds, buying wool to be sent by packhorse to London, from where it was shipped to Calais and Bruges. In November 1478 Richard Cely wrote, 'I have bought of William Midwinter of Northleach 40 sacks of good Cotswold wool, good wool and middle wool of the same 40 sacks, price the sack of both good wool and middle wool 12 marks [£8]'. Sales in Bruges were so good the next year that Richard Cely bought 97 sacks, and again in 1481 George Cely, who was the family agent abroad, pressed his father to buy as

28 *John Fortey (d.1459).*

29 *The house of William Grevel, 'the flower of the wool merchants of all England', Chipping Campden.*

30 *A Cotswold wool-man. The memorial brass at Northleach to John Taylor and his wife, Joan, c.1490.*

much as possible. Richard explained the difficulties, replying that 'wool in Cotswold is at great price 13s. 4d. [66p] a tod [28 lbs or 12.7 kilos], and great riding for wool in Cotswold as was any year this seven years'.

Farther south, Cirencester had 10 wool merchants in 1341, and at Fairford another great merchant family had their home. John Tame, who died in 1500, bought the manor and rebuilt the church, adorning it with some of the best 15th-century stained glass surviving in the country. The great size of some of the market squares of Cotswold towns, like Cirencester, Northleach and Stow (all later partly built over), was to accommodate the gatherings at the sheep sales, though it is unlikely that medieval sales attained the scale of the 18th-century Stow fairs when 20,000 sheep were sold.

Although the demand abroad for English wool was maintained, exports steadily dropped as cloth was increasingly manufactured in this country. The change of emphasis is seen in the export figures. About half came from the West Country mills, which made all the broad cloths. This was a heavier cloth than the East Anglian worsteds, and required fulling, a process in which the cloth is beaten in water to make it thick and felted. Plenty of good water is needed, therefore, preferably with a local supply of soapy fuller's earth.

Although there is abundant evidence of the widespread distribution of fulling mills along rural streams from 1300, the early cloth-making industry was centred chiefly in the towns. In this activity Bristol held an advantage as a port from which both wool and cloth was shipped direct to the Continent, especially after 1297, the year that Edward I introduced a tax on wool exports. Bristol then became one of the ports with a customs officer through which the trade was channelled. Before 1339 Thomas Blanket had established a large-scale weaving shop, though not without opposition. The Weavers', Dyers' and Fullers' guilds issued complex rules for the protection of their members and to ensure that good work was done by the craftsmen. Manufacture had to be carried out within the city, and in public sight, not in back rooms. Prices and wages were controlled, together with regulations for the purchase and sale of cloth. In Gloucester, Tewkesbury and Cirencester similar guilds were not chartered until Tudor reigns, although those towns contained clothiers and craftsmen from the 13th century. In the 15th century 'Gloucester

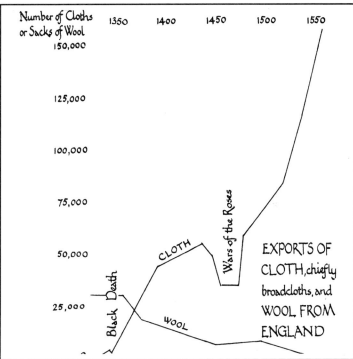

Reds' were already well known, forerunners of the even more famous 18th-century 'Stroud Scarlets'. The smaller Cotswold towns were also clothing centres, but the need for good water power and the desire of landowners to turn their own wool into cloth encouraged them to build or convert rural watermills wherever there were suitable conditions.

Such conditions were to be found on the fast-flowing streams of the Stroud valleys. Even before the end of the 12th century there were four fullers in Minchinhampton, a parish which stretched from Chalford in one valley to Nailsworth in another. A century later there were seven mills there and more in the neighbouring villages of Rodborough and Woodchester. Others were scattered elsewhere in the Cotswolds. There was a fulling mill at Temple Guiting in 1185, at Bourton-on-the-Water in 1206, and at Stanway later in the 13th century. At Hawkesbury the tenants were fined if they took wool to be fulled at any mill other than their lord's and the abbot of Winchcombe fined his Sherborne tenants in 1341 for attempting to set up a fulling mill in competition with his own. But the later concentration of the industry in the villages near Stroud was clearly evident by the mid-15th century, and in 1557 its importance was so well established that an Act of Parliament, restricting cloth manufacture to towns only, specifically exempted 'any towns or villages near the River Stroud in the county of Gloucester, where cloths have been made for twenty years past'.

31 (above left) *Chipping Campden church and almshouses. Wealthy cloth merchants transformed the church from c.1450. The almshouses were built by Sir Baptist Hicks in 1612.*

32 (above) *Graph showing exports of cloth and wool.*

6

Early Bristol

33 *St John's conduit.*

So far as is known the town took no part in the resistance offered to the Norman Conqueror. William adopted the policy of replacing Englishmen by Normans in high official posts. Therefore, he placed Bristol under the charge of a Norman noble, Geoffrey of Mowbray, bishop of Coutances, who strengthened the town by building the first fortification on the narrow strip of land to the east of the town, the only unprotected side. At that time the town occupied an area of about 30 acres and was almost encircled by the Rivers Avon and Frome. After the death of Geoffrey, the castle and borough passed to one of the most powerful of Norman lords, Robert FitzHamon, and upon his death this great inheritance passed by marriage to Robert, Earl of Gloucester. Earl Robert made Bristol a main centre of his power. Strong as Geoffrey's castle was held to be, Robert rebuilt it on a grand scale, building a great stone keep, enclosing the whole with massive walls and bastions. The castle became a royal stronghold dominating the town most effectively until the close of the 14th century. A chronicler of that time states 'that the town was almost the richest in the country owing to its foreign and domestic trade, while its castle, standing on a mighty mound was garrisoned by crowds of knights and soldiers'. This fortress had scarcely been finished before it became the scene of revolt against King Stephen, which was not surprising since Robert was one of the most powerful supporters of the Empress Matilda in the struggle for the throne.

On to this scene emerged Robert FitzHarding as a person of great importance in the town. He held the office of reeve at a time when the Empress Matilda and her son Henry were living in the castle under the protection of Earl Robert. FitzHarding was their loyal friend and supporter, placing his wealth at their disposal. He owned a number of manors in Gloucestershire and from Earl Robert bought the manor of Billeswick which lay outside the town walls. It was here that he founded the abbey of Augustinian Canons, the church of which, after the Dissolution, became the cathedral church of Bristol. In 1154, the newly crowned Henry II bestowed on Robert FitzHarding the forfeited estates of Roger of Berkeley and these gifts enabled FitzHarding to build in a more elaborate style.

At this time Bristol was a royal manor and, as reeve of the town, FitzHarding was the royal official appointed to govern the town and to collect the rents and dues. With the growing power of the burgesses (that

36

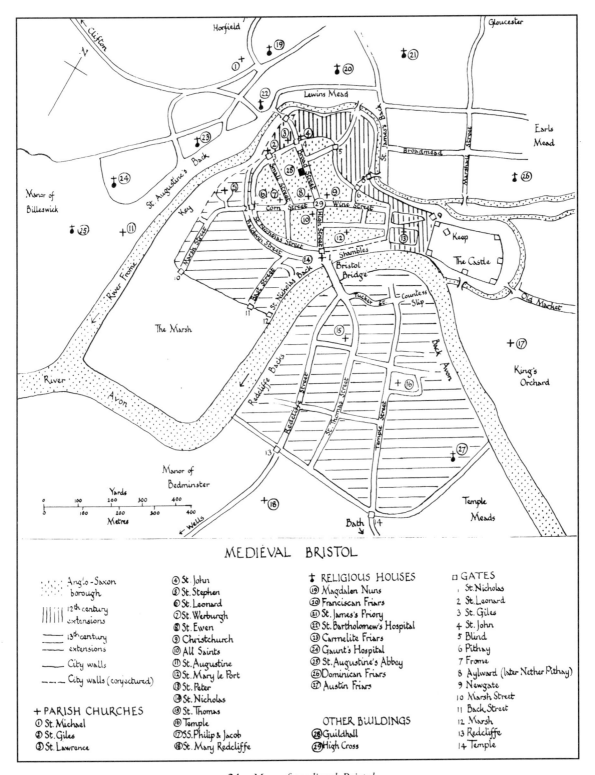

34 *Map of medieval Bristol.*

35 *St John's Gateway, Broad Street, Bristol. The last remaining medieval gate of the city.*

is, the householders holding their shops, houses and gardens of the lord), the building of the castle and the increasing wealth from successful trading, the borough began to establish a separate official life. At the beginning of the 13th century the burgesses were given the right to choose their own mayor and the old manorial rule gave way to communal government. By the 14th century, Bristol was the chief port of the west. It was at this time that the town attained the most complete measure of self government, securing, first among provincial boroughs, the full jurisdiction and status of a corporate county. The townsmen were now to a large extent independent of the king and more particularly of the king's officials in the castle.

The map (p.37) shows the principal features of medieval Bristol. The town was enclosed by walls, pierced by a number of gates. Many of the gates were crowned by churches, of which St John's survives as a typical example. At the intersection of the four main streets stood the High Cross (now to be seen at Stourhead in Wiltshire) which was a focus of civil and religious ceremonies. Here the bellman cried aloud to the passers-by to pray for the souls of the founders and benefactors of the adjoining churches on the days of their commemoration; here also, kings and queens were received, proclamations read and vagrants whipped. Round the High Cross stood three of Bristol's oldest churches: All Saints, Christchurch and St Ewen. Seated in the window of St Ewen's church, Edward IV watched his enemy Sir Baldwin Fulford pass to his execution at the High Cross.

Every evening at eight o'clock the curfew rang from the towers of St Nicholas and St Werburgh. The curfew bell spoke to the medieval town as a unit of organised government and its tone brought a sense of rest and security. It was a signal for the closing of shops and taverns, and marked the setting of the night watch.

The roads which followed the line of the walls still preserve the shape of the early town. It was a small town judged by our standards, and as the population increased from about 3,000 at the time of the Conquest to 10,000 by the end of the 15th century, largely immigrants from places within forty miles, it must have become very constricted. Beyond the walls on the northern side of the town was a ring of religious houses so that it was impossible for the town to extend its boundaries until the break-up of the monastic estates in the 16th century. On the south side of the River Avon was the manor of Bedminster owned by the Berkeley family. That part of it, near Bristol Bridge, which had become

36 *Bristol High Cross.*

a thriving urban area due to the development of the cloth industry, was brought within the town in the 13th century. There were houses outside the gates near the Old Market, in the vicinity of St James Priory and around the Abbey of St Augustine. The city boundaries as defined by its charter of 1373 extended even further beyond the walls, taking in districts known as St Augustine, St Michael, St James, St Philip and Jacob, and Redcliffe, and the water of the Avon and Severn as far as the Steep and Flat Holms.

The streets of the town were narrow, steep and in common with most of England in a bad condition. The maintenance of paving the roads was the responsibility of the owners of the frontages of the houses. About 1565, John Willy, city chamberlain, earned the gratitude of his fellow citizens for the effort he made in repairing the main streets. It is recorded 'John Willy, the best chamberlain that ever was in Bristol, who being a merchant built the Mermaid in Brodestreat and after that he set men to work, and caused all the causeways to be 7 miles everyway about this city, most at his own charge'. The duty of clearing up the streets was done by one man, known as the 'raker', who in the first instance depended upon the goodwill of the householders, but afterwards was paid by the Council 18d. (7$\frac{1}{2}$p) per week. The townsmen enjoyed one of the best water supplies in the country and for this they were indebted to the friars who bore the initial cost of laying the pipes, whilst the maintenance was paid for by bequests from grateful citizens.

37 *Part of Bristol Bridge.*

The Carmelites, whose house stood on the site of the Colston Hall, granted to the parishioners of St John's a 'feather' from their pipe of water which came from a spring on Brandon Hill. The water still runs to the cistern adjoining St John's Church. Provided by wells and conduits, it was more than adequate for the population of that time. Water had to be fetched by the inhabitants from the conduits and wells. People of all ages carrying every kind of vessel, making their way to the sources of supply, were a common sight. For those who could afford to buy water, the water carriers made a business of selling it. For industrial and cleansing purposes the rivers were a valuable source of water.

The religious and social guilds were the centre of the social life of the town. In Bristol there were some thirty guilds bringing together men and women of particular crafts, each with its hall and a chapel dedicated to its patron saint within the parish church. The halls of the bakers, cutlers and coopers still survive. The street names reveal the sites of many of the crafts. The fullers and tuckers gave their name to Tucker Street, the cutlers lived in Knifesmith Street, the butchers had their shambles in 'Bocherew' and the cooks had shops in Cook Row, where in 1470 six cooks were trading. Regulations ensured that they sold wholesome food. If a cook sold warmed-up flesh or pork he was fined 3s. 4d. [16$\frac{1}{2}$p].

7

Bristol Merchants

In spite of the collapse of the wars with France and the misery of the War of the Roses, the latter half of the 15th century was a great time for Bristol.

The mercantile life of the town was vigorous and prosperous. The wharves and cellars were piled high with cloth and hogsheads of wine. Many ships brought up the Avon large cargoes from France, Spain, Iceland and elsewhere. Trade flowed in and out of the town by land and sea. Bristol drew on a wide inland area for the commodities which she exported. Among the leading merchants were men such as Robert Sturmy, William Canynges and John Shipward. The custom accounts show that Robert Sturmy carried cargoes of wool, tin, cloth and lead to the Levant, where they were exchanged for oriental spices and other luxuries. John Shipward sent cloth, beans and barrels of herrings to Bordeaux and brought back from Spain wine and iron, oil and tar, such delicacies as saffron, almonds, liquorice and vinegar. He was also engaged in trade with Iceland and on one occasion sent his ship the *Christopher of Bristol* laden with a varied and interesting cargo:

'20 weys of salt, 12 lasts of flour, 4 barrels of honey, 8 weys of malt, 80 dozen cloth without grain, 200 horseshoes, 6 full cooking pots, 6 gross of unlined caps, locks, girdles, flanders linen, combs, purses, 500 needles, 8 pounds of thread and $1/2$ pound of silk.' This trade with Iceland must have been the toughest and most venturesome part of Bristol maritime enterprise but, at this time, commerce was an adventure rather than a speculation.

William Canynges is traditionally the merchant prince and ship-owner *par excellence* of 15th-century Bristol. In 1460 he owned nine ships, employed 800 seamen and 100 other workmen. For his time, Canynges's fleet was impressive. But he was not alone, for in 1480 Thomas Strange owned 12 vessels. Women also took part in the busy commercial life of Bristol. Alice Chester, after the death of her husband in 1474, carried on with success his business of importing iron from Spain and sending cloth to Lisbon and Flanders. She owned several ships and out of the profits of the trade she had built the first public crane on the quay.

These wealthy merchants lived in large and comfortable houses. John Shipward lived in a fine mansion house near St Stephen's Church

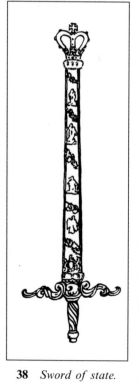

38 *Sword of state.*

and within easy reach of the quay. From his house he conducted his day-to-day business. In the cellars, which were often of massive construction with groined and ribbed roofs extending under the streets, the merchandise was stored. The mansion house of Robert Sturmy with its adjoining cloth hall was one of the finest buildings in the town. Here, he kept open house for 'foreign merchants and gentlemen of Bristol to the great benefit of commerce'. William of Worcester writing in 1480 describes Canynges's house as having a tower of great beauty, and being ornamented with bay-windows. Here, he entertained Edward IV in 1461. The contract for the rebuilding of Alice Chester's house in High Street shows that it was four storeys high. Above the ground floor shop was a hall with one of the new oriel windows, above this another chamber with an oriel window.

Much of the information about the personal lives of these men comes from wills and inventories of their possessions. From them can be learnt something of the state and splendour of their private lives, the richness of their clothing and the comfort of their homes. The sumptuary laws they disregarded until Henry VII fined the merchants of Bristol 'because their wives so finely dressed'. The effigy of Edmond Blanket in St Stephen's Church shows the characteristic dress of the wealthy merchant at the end of the 14th century. He wears a 'cote hardie' over a tunic with tight sleeves. On the shoulders he has a small falling cape fastened in front. The legs are covered with close-fitting hose and the feet with sandals. Below the waist he wears a handsome jewelled belt which shows him to have been a person of importance and substantial means, for the sumptuary laws of Edward III forbade the use of such belts to anyone under the rank of a knight unless he was possessed of £200. These newly rich merchants were not in the least ashamed of their origins—indeed they were proud to commemorate in their shields and merchant marks the wool packs, or wine casks or tools that had brought them prosperity.

39 *St Stephen's Tower, Bristol.*

The government of the town was almost entirely in the hands of the merchants. They also represented the town in Parliament. John Shipward and his family were one of the many merchant families who amassed a substantial fortune and built up a position in society. He served as a bailiff, sheriff and was four times mayor of Bristol. His son was sheriff and mayor and one of the king's collectors of customs. William Canynges was twice member of Parliament and mayor no less than five times.

With the combination of business acumen and religious fervour that characterises the medieval mind, it was this merchant prince who contributed largely to the rebuilding of St Mary Redcliffe. Planned like a cathedral, Queen Elizabeth I when she visited Bristol in 1574 called it the 'fairest, goodliest, and most perfect parish church in England'. In 1467 Canynges gave up all his worldly possessions to become a priest. When he entered the priesthood, he sang his first mass at St Mary Redcliffe, and this is commemorated every Whitsuntide by the Rush Sunday service. The floor of the chancel is strewn with rushes, a medieval fashion, and the Lord Mayor and Corporation attend the service in

40 *St Mary Redcliffe church, Bristol. Mostly 14th-century and described by Queen Elizabeth I as 'the fairest, goodliest, and most perfect parish church in England'.*

full civic dress. Each is given a posy of flowers, a relic of the days when bunches of sweet smelling herbs were used as a precaution against infectious diseases.

During the later Middle Ages those merchants whose main interest was in foreign trade banded themselves together in a Fellowship of Merchants, through which they were able to regulate the trade of the town. It is likely that this body later became the Society of Merchant Venturers of Bristol.

Several fairs and markets were held in Bristol. The fair of St James was among the most famous and must have brought great revenue to the priory of St James. Every year at the Feast of Pentecost, the fair drew merchants from all over Europe to buy and sell in Bristol. In the porch of the priory was held the Piepowder Court ('the court of the dusty feet') where all the disputes of the fair were settled. To the fairs flocked the trader with his wares, the merchant to renew his shop, and retail buyers for their humble needs. There, with the corn, the skins, the wool, the fish and meat from the country were to be seen wines, oils, fruits, iron from Spain, spices from Alexandria, silks, velvets and glass from Venice, hardwoods, spices, wax, woad and salt from Lisbon. At the fair, traders and pilgrims combined religious devotion with worldly business and entertainment. The bishop of Worcester granted indulgences to all who should visit St James's at fair time and give alms in the church, where was enshrined some precious relic. Showmen of all kinds, wrestlers, bearwards, conjurors and ballad singers, whose ware was often of a ribald type, gave pleasure to the thronging crowds.

41 *Merchant Venturers' arms.*

8

Medieval Market Towns

The medieval wool and cloth trade in Gloucestershire certainly encouraged the growth of many towns, but few owed their foundation solely to this cause. Stroud and Nailsworth are examples of towns that grew unaided at the natural centres for cloth-making at a comparatively late date. Most of the Gloucestershire towns either developed at ancient sites of strategic or commercial importance, like Gloucester and Tewkesbury, or were deliberately established by landowners to attract trade, and therefore improve the prosperity of their estates, like Wotton-under-Edge and Thornbury. In some cases a completely new town was carved out of a rural manor, as at Chipping Sodbury, Stow and Northleach, and sometimes part of a village was set aside for development as a borough, as at New Street in Painswick and the Burgage in Prestbury. Size is no indication of former borough status, for today the casual observer would not recognise Leonard Stanley, Dymock or Wickwar as 'towns'.

The features which differentiated a town from an ordinary village included the right to hold a fair, perhaps more than once a year, and a weekly market, the freedom of the townsmen from agricultural services, separate law courts, special officials such as mayor and aldermen, and

42 *Thornbury. Elegant 18th-century frontages mingle with older gabled buildings in the main streets.*

43 *Newent became a borough in 1253. Its timber-framed market hall dates from* c.*1600.*

44 *Gloucester cross.*

freedom from all manorial tolls and dues. A successful town site needed good communications and a reasonably large surrounding rural area to attract custom. Although Dymock had 66 burgesses in the early 13th century, it failed because it was too near Newent, which lay on a more important route from Wales, and Prestbury suffered from the proximity of Cheltenham. The map (p.45) shows that the medieval market towns were remarkably evenly distributed at about ten miles distance from each other, which was also a convenient daily riding distance for itinerant traders. Gloucester, Tewkesbury and Newnham grew at river crossings, and cross-road sites were chosen for Northleach, Newent and Stow.

In appearance many ancient market towns contain features in common. Large new market places adjoining the main thoroughfare were laid out at Wotton-under-Edge, Northleach and Tetbury. At Cirencester and Stow temporary stalls became permanent buildings which restricted the open area, those at Cirencester being removed in 1830. Similarly the row of shops and church which stood in the centre of Westgate Street in Gloucester was demolished in the 18th century, to ease traffic congestion. The broad streets of Chipping Campden and Moreton-in-Marsh are less confined, and at Chipping Sodbury the old road was deliberately diverted to make a market street. The market houses set on pillars with shaded shelter below for the sale of dairy produce and public rooms above, which are such an attractive feature of towns like Dursley and Minchinhampton, are of 17th- and 18th-century construction. They replaced market crosses, and a town as small as Mitcheldean had four called the Market Cross, the High Cross, the Merend Cross and the Butter Cross.

Among the features of any ancient town are the long and narrow-fronted burgage plots of equal size, which commonly run from the main street to a back lane. Despite the amalgamation of plots in the subsequent rebuilding of houses, shops and supermarkets, they may still he identified in places as diverse as Cheltenham and Marshfield. The plan of Wotton-under-Edge is even more regular for in 1253 Katherine Lady Berkeley established a completely new town with a formal layout on a grid pattern.

Gloucester was by far the most important all the towns except Bristol. Most of the houses lay in the part leading towards the river quays and castle. Before 1200 Northgate Street was the market place. Later, Westgate Street became the most important street and contained the

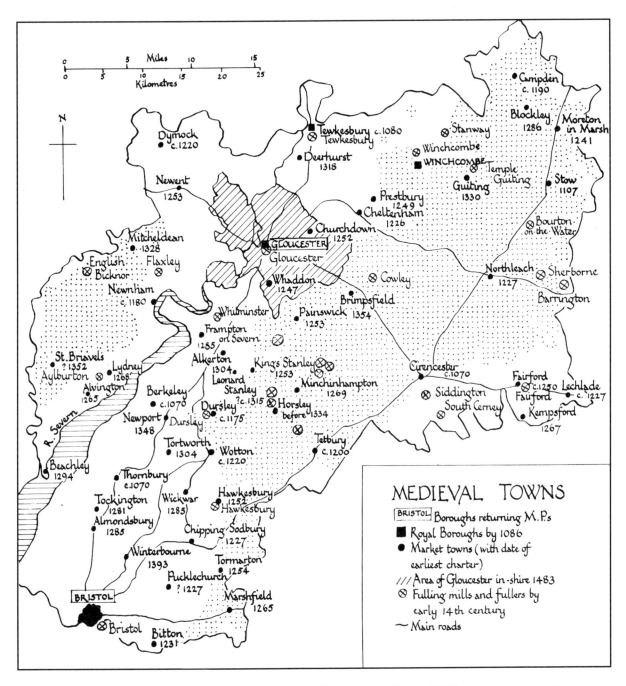

MEDIEVAL TOWNS

BRISTOL Boroughs returning M.P.s
■ Royal Boroughs by 1086
● Market towns (with date of earliest charter)
/// Area of Gloucester in-shire 1483
⊗ Fulling mills and fullers by early 14th century
— Main roads

Booth Hall, the medieval market and town hall recorded from 1230 on the site of the later Shire Hall. The great Midsummer Fair, held for a whole week in Westgate Street, was the only occasion when traders were not obliged to conduct their business at either the Booth Hall or in the shops of the burgesses. Barton Fair at the end of September had been

45 *Medieval towns.*

granted to Gloucester Abbey in 1227, but was held outside the walls, and it survives today as a pleasure fair as do some of the mop fairs of the country towns. Stretching up Westgate Street in the mid-15th century were the stalls of the butchery, mercery and herb and fish markets. Leather workers were concentrated near the High Cross in Northgate and Southgate Streets, and metal workers of all sorts—smiths, wiredrawers, bell-founders and goldsmiths—were grouped behind Westgate Street in Longsmith Street and Berkeley (formerly Broadsmith) Street. The old name of Lower Quay Street was Fuller's or Walker's Lane, recalling the cloth workers, and in Eastgate Street there was a Jewish quarter. The whole bustling town was protected by its Norman walls built on the Roman foundations. The maintenance of the walls was a heavy charge on the townspeople, so a royal charter of 1345 gave them the right to levy tolls to pay for the cost. Ten years earlier by another charter the town was allowed to collect customs duties on ships' cargoes, honey, wool and iron to pay for paving the town. Already in the Middle Ages there was a busy grain trade with France and Ireland.

A town as large and important as Gloucester had a well-organised administration. Its earliest charter of liberties was granted in 1155 by Henry II, who 15 years later suppressed an attempt by the citizens to claim greater self government. Such rights came only from the king. In 1483 a further charter permitted the election of a mayor, sheriff and coroner, and the establishment of city law courts; by the same charter the city was granted a great tract of countryside to form the 'in-shire' of the county of the city of Gloucester. Soon afterwards the earliest recorded bye-laws were drawn up. Bakers, brewers, butchers and fishmongers were required to sell lawful quantities of good quality, while for cleanliness 'no swyne nor dukkes goo in the opon stretes', and 'non person nor

46   Cirencester, 1804. The houses in the market place were demolished in 1830. The church with its three-storey porch is in the background.

persons wesshe non tubbes nother barels for ale nother non other fylthy vessels att the Hight Crosse'. Because the town had earned a bad reputation there were severe penalties against immorality, those found guilty being paraded around the town in an open cart as part of their punishment.

Similar bye-laws were enforced in the smaller towns, although their administration was much simpler. At Northleach the bye-laws of 1576 controlled the election of officials, procedure at meetings, and settlement of debts. Townsmen could be fined for playing games, keeping unlicensed inns, and receiving strange paupers into their homes, while people who wandered about the town at night were punished by putting them 'in the common stocks by the heels all that night'.

The guilds had a special function in the larger towns. At Gloucester all the merchants were members of the Guild Merchant, even if they were not always burgesses. They regulated all general commercial affairs from the Booth Hall. In addition they would also have been members of their craft guild, of which there were at least twenty in the Middle Ages. During every Midsummer Fair week they held a lavish festival, processing with their colourful silk banners through the streets, messy with garbage and crowded with bystanders, where the raucous cries of salesmen and pedlars competed with the clattering of carts and noise of wandering animals.

9
Churches and Monasteries

The Norman Conquest was followed by ecclesiastical, as well as political and social, changes. Normans replaced Saxons as bishops, administrative reforms were introduced, and the invaders began a tremendous programme of building new churches, both monastic and parochial. Wulstan, the Saxon bishop of Worcester (d.1095) was allowed to remain in office, unlike most of his countrymen, because of his loyalty to both William I and William II, and because of his saintly reputation, which led to his canonisation (his saint's day being 19 January). He taught and preached throughout his large diocese, one of his most notable achievements being the successful suppression of the Bristol slave trade to Ireland.

Within his diocese many parish churches were rebuilt. All the surviving ancient churches are built of stone, which usually could be dug locally, although for Tewkesbury Abbey stone was brought all the way by sea and river from Normandy itself. Very few Norman churches have remained unchanged except in small and remote villages. At Stoke Orchard near Tewkesbury is one such simple church. It was built about 1170 and decorated a few years later with wall-paintings showing the life of its patron saint, St James of Compostella. The slightly older wall-paintings at Kempley are even more remarkable. In the low, brightly coloured Norman chancel are full-length portraits, including probably the builders of the church, Walter de Lacy, William the Conqueror's loyal supporter, and his son Hugh. Norman carvings and sculpture abound in Gloucestershire churches, especially those of the smaller Cotswold villages like Elkstone and Quenington, but in most places a growing population later demanded larger and richer churches. Perhaps the most distinc-

48 *Bristol Cathedral. The Norman chapter house. Engraving by E. Blore, 1824.*

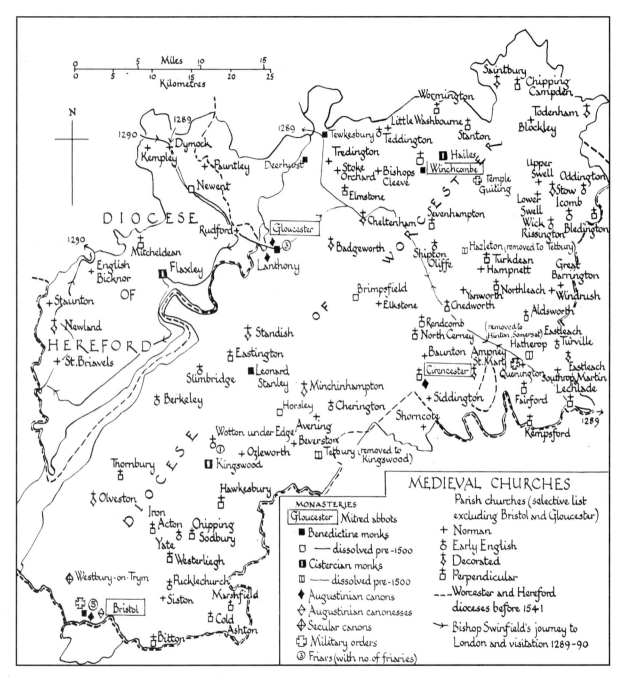

Miles 10 15
Kilometres 20 25

N

DIOCESE

OF

HEREFORD

OF WORCESTER

DIOCESE

1289
1290
1289
1289
1290

Saintbury
Chipping Campden
Wormington
Todenham
Little Washbourne
Blockley
Tewkesbury
Teddington
Stanton
Tredington
Hailes
Upper Swell
Oddington
Stoke Orchard
Bishops Cleeve
Winchcombe
Temple Guiting
Stow
Icomb
Dymock
Kempley
Pauntley
Deerhurst
Elmstone
Lower Swell
Bledington
Newent
Cheltenham
Sevenhampton
Wick Rissington
Mitcheldean
Rudford
Gloucester
Lanthony
Badgeworth
Shipton Oliffe
Hazleton (removed to Tetbury)
Great Barrington
English Bicknor
Flaxley
Brimpsfield
Turkdean
Hampnett
Windrush
Staunton
Elkstone
Yanworth
Northleach
Aldsworth
Newland
Chedworth
St.Briavels
Standish
Rendcomb
North Cerney
(removed to Hinton,Somerset) Eastleach
Hatherop
Turville
Eastington
Baunton
Ampney St.Mary
Eastleach Martin
Leonard Stanley
Cirencester
Quenington
Southrop
Lechlade
Slimbridge
Minchinhampton
Berkeley
Horsley
Cherington
Siddington
Fairford
Shorncote
1289
Avening
Wotton under Edge
Beverston
Kempsford
Ozleworth
Tetbury (removed to Kingswood)
Kingswood
Thornbury
Hawkesbury
Olveston
Iron Acton
Chipping Sodbury
Yate
Westerleigh
Westbury-on-Trym
Rucklechurch
Marshfield
Bristol
Siston
Cold Ashton
Bitton

MONASTERIES
Gloucester Mitred abbots
■ Benedictine monks
□ — dissolved pre-1500
◨ Cistercian monks
◩ — dissolved pre-1500
◆ Augustinian canons
◇ Augustinian canonesses
◈ Secular canons
✠ Military orders
③ Friars (with no. of friaries)

MEDIEVAL CHURCHES
Parish churches (selective list excluding Bristol and Gloucester)
+ Norman
ð Early English
✧ Decorated
ð Perpendicular
--- Worcester and Hereford dioceses before 1541
↳ Bishop Swinfield's journey to London and visitation 1289-90

tive feature raised by succeeding generations was the 14th-century fashion for tall, narrow spires in churches in the Vale and at the foot of the
Cotswolds. In Bristol very little now remains of the work of the Norman
builders, where in the Middle Ages there were 18 parish churches and
several non-parochial churches. Every one of them was rebuilt in the

49 *Medieval churches.*

14th and 15th centuries when local patriotism prompted the wealthy merchants to rebuild and endow them. Others were refashioned during Bristol's second period of prosperity in the 18th century.

In the same manner the wealth of the medieval Cotswold wool merchants was partly spent in lavishly rebuilding churches in the latest style. The Perpendicular churches at Chipping Campden, Fairford and Northleach, adorned with the brass memorials to their benefactors, are outstanding, but spectacular in every respect is the great Perpendicular and Tudor parish church built by the abbots and merchants of Cirencester (illustration 46). From the outside the most striking features are the three-storey porch, built by the abbot for offices and business premises, and the tower, unfinished and lacking its spire because the foundations settled too much. Inside, the lofty nave is so impressive that it is easy to forget that much of the history of the town is to be sought in the smaller details—the trade marks of the merchants and clothiers which decorate the nave and chapels, the elaborate brasses and monuments of merchants and squires and their fashion-conscious wives, the figure of the

50 *Gloucester Cathedral cloisters, c.1351-1412, contain the earliest fan-vaulting known. In this south walk are the monks' study carrels.*

Bluecoat schoolboy asking for alms, and the sculpture of the merry Whitsun Ale procession on the stringcourse of the outside wall of the nave.

The failing Saxon monasteries were also revitalised by the Normans. Under abbot Serlo (1072-1104) Gloucester Abbey was rebuilt, and the nave arcade and crypt still survive from his time. The abbey was the scene of great events—William the Conqueror ordering the compilation of Domesday Book in 1085, the hasty coronation of Henry III, and the Parliament of 1378, when the monks complained that 'the convent was obliged by necessity for some days while Parliament lasted to take their meals in the dormitory, and afterwards in the schoolroom ... . All open spaces in the monastery were so crowded by persons coming to the Parliament that they appeared more like a fair than a house of religion.

The grass in the cloister was so trampled down with wrestling and foot-ball playing, that not a vestige of green was to be seen upon it.' The Lords sat in the newly-built great hall, and the Commons in the chapter house, the sessions being notable for the confirmation of the Statute of Labourers regulating wages, and an attack by Wyclif on the right of sanctuary. Parliaments also met at Gloucester in 1278 and 1407.

The members of the Parliament in 1378 would have been able to admire the great east window of the abbey church, which was a memorial to the knights who fell at the battle of Crécy in 1346 during the Hundred Years' War. Later, before setting out for the Agincourt campaign in 1415, Henry V made a pilgrimage to Gloucester. The king was perhaps the most famous of the pilgrims who according to tradition flocked to the church to make their homage at the tomb of Edward II, brutally murdered at Berkeley Castle in 1327. The pilgrims' gifts and the wealth of its landed estates enabled the abbey to rebuild its church in the early 15th century as the earliest large-scale venture in Perpendicular architecture.

Other new foundations by the Normans included the great Bene-dictine houses of Tewkesbury (1102) and St Augustine's, Bristol (1142-8). Tewkesbury Abbey had a cell, or dependent convent, in Bristol called St James's Priory. This was founded by Robert Earl of Gloucester at the same time that he was building the great keep of Bristol Castle, that is, between 1129 and 1137. Tradition has it that Earl Robert set aside every tenth stone in the construction of the castle to build this church. This may well be so, for it was not unusual in those days for men who were distinguished soldiers to set off their military achievements by making gifts to the church or founding some religious house. The monks of Llanthony Priory in the Black Mountains on the Welsh border were given a safer home just outside Gloucester by Miles Earl of Hereford in 1136, and a century later another great warrior, Richard Earl of Corn-wall, founded Hailes Abbey as a thank-offering for his preservation dur-ing a storm at sea. The monasteries attracted gifts of estates and posses-sions from pious men in all ranks of society and so became wealthy institutions, often lacking the religious zeal that had characterised their early years.

Later in the Middle Ages the friars won an effective influence largely because they chose to live in the town centres and remained poor and landless. The Dominicans founded their friary at Bristol in 1227-8, and were followed soon afterwards by the Franciscans and Carmelites. Hos-pitals for the care of the sick and aged were provided by various mem-bers of the Berkeley family. The largest was St Mark's founded in 1220 by a grandson of Robert FitzHarding and there one hundred poor were fed daily. Outside the walls of the town were hospitals, for leprous men and women. There were similar houses at Gloucester, where the Domini-can friary founded in 1239 is still virtually complete.

The bishops of Worcester and Hereford remained active in their pastoral work. Wulstan de Bransford was bishop of Worcester when the Black Death spread from the south coast in 1348-9. Conditions were worst in Bristol but throughout the diocese many clergy caught the disease. At North Cerney two rectors died in the course of the year and in Gloucestershire 80 livings had to be filled during the summer. Wulstan de Bransford dutifully rode the length of his diocese, instituting new clergy to serve the stricken countryside where a quarter to a third of the population died, until he at last succumbed to the plague himself, and died in August at his palace at Hartlebury in Worcestershire.

The Black Death must have contributed to the shortage of priests, and later in the century the bishop of Hereford found that the Forest was poorly served. At Pauntley and Woolaston the parsons were non-resident, discipline lax, and churches were in poor repair. At Dymock the roof was so bad 'that when it rains hard the vicar cannot celebrate Mass'. Such shortcomings encouraged the spread of Lollard doctrines of John Wyclif and his supporters, and they became strong in both the Forest of Dean and Bristol. Conditions in Bristol were exceptionally favourable, a large manufacturing city with many poor artisans on the extreme limit of the diocese. Wyclif's disciple, John Purvey, settled there about 1384 and won such a great influence over the weavers and other artisans that forty marched to join the Lollard revolt of 1414. Even after the suppression of the movement Lollard traditions lingered in the city for the rest of the century. One of Wyclif's associates in Oxford had been John Trevisa (d. 1402), who while vicar of Berkeley made a French translation of the Bible. A hundred years later reform was encouraged by an early English translation of the Bible by William Tyndale, born in or near Stinchcombe and tutor in Sir John Walsh's household at Little Sodbury about 1520.

The Reformation had far-reaching local effects. The monasteries were closed and destroyed between 1536 and 1540. Some churches were preserved—Gloucester and Bristol became the cathedral churches for the new dioceses created in 1541 and 1542, while Tewkesbury was bought by the town for £453 as a parish church. Others were completely razed. The Cistercian abbey at Hailes was a particular target of the reformers' attack. In 1270 Edmund Earl of Cornwall had given the monastery a phial reputed to contain a small quantity of the blood of Christ. Pilgrims had for centuries flocked to the convent to venerate such an extraordinary relic. Now Henry VIII's zealous officials seized the famous blood, and on 29 October 1538 bishop Hugh Latimer of Worcester wrote to Thomas Cromwell, 'We have been boulting and sifting the blood of Hayles all this forenoon ... . And verily it seemeth to be an unctuous gum and compound of many things'. After the valuables were removed the deserted monastery was rifled by local folk, including the servants of Robert Acton, the sheriff of Worcestershire and first tenant of the monastic buildings. He himself silenced one of his women servants who remonstrated, 'Hold thy peace, for it is there now: Catch that may catch!' The estates were disposed of in a typical manner. The Crown kept them for a short time, before selling them to a speculator who bought up great lots of former monastic property. He also soon split his gains and sold them,

51 *Iron Acton cross, a memorial probably to Robert Poyntz (d.1439).*

52 *Hailes Abbey. The remaining cloisters seen across the church after the abbey was used as a quarry following its dissolution in 1539.*

and eventually, about 1600, the site of Hailes Abbey was acquired by a local squire, Sir John Tracy. As for the monks, the new cathedrals of Gloucester and Bristol had bishops and deans who had been abbots or priors and other monks became parish clergy or received pensions.

In the parishes the new services, destruction of medieval church furnishings and removal of chantry chapels were for the most part quietly accepted. In a few places a conservative parson delayed change, as at Minchinhampton until 1570. At Tewkesbury the miracle plays survived until 1600 and there is little evidence of that iconoclasm which led the vicar of Tidenham to smash his stained glass in 1548. Most of the changes in Gloucester were delayed until the election of the Puritan John Hooper as bishop in 1551. In two years this energetic man had stirred up his apathetic or ignorant clergy. Some were so badly qualified that they could not recite the Commandments or, like the vicar of South Cerney, believed that the Lord's Prayer was so called because it 'was given by his lord the King and written in the King's book of Common Prayer'. But Hooper's reforms were short-lived. On Mary's accession he was arrested, tried, and brought to Gloucester to be burnt outside his own cathedral in 1555.

10

Discovery and Exploration

At the end of the 15th century—the dawn of the age of discovery—Bristol was already a great port. Bristol men in search of trade had dared the seas in small ships and by their successful ventures had established trade with Spain and Portugal and even Iceland. Through this close association with the Iberian peninsula and Iceland, Bristol became familiar with much legendary information about the lands to the westward. The idea was firmly fixed in the minds of the merchants that there was an island called Brasylle to the west of Ireland, and Bristol sailors returning from Iceland brought stories of the 'Western Isles' and the 'Island of Brazil'. The merchants were excited by these stories and in 1480 a remarkable venture was launched from Bristol. Twelve years before Columbus, John Jay with a ship of 80 tons set out to find the island of Brazil. After nine weeks' search in the Atlantic they were driven back to Ireland and so ended the first known attempt made by the citizens of Bristol to discover new lands to the westward. Although little is known about subsequent expeditions, it is certain that others were sponsored by Bristol merchants. This zeal for exploration may well have been the reason why John Cabot, a citizen of Venice, came to Bristol. He must have been a remarkable person, for in the short time that he was in Bristol he was able to win the confidence of the powerful merchants of his day and persuade them to equip and finance an expedition which he was prepared to lead.

53 *The* Matthew.

On 2 May 1497, John Cabot in a small ship, the *Matthew*, with a crew of 18 men, sailed out from Bristol harbour across the unknown Atlantic on a voyage longer and more perilous than that ever undertaken before; but it was the sea trail of the Northmen they followed. On 14 June, after 52 days at sea, they sighted land, drew in to shore, disembarked and hoisted the flags of England and St Mark on an unknown soil, claiming this 'new found land' for the king of England. John Cabot returned to Bristol to announce that he had found the 'mainland of Cathay, the territory of the Grand Khan'; he had, in fact, found the mainland of North America for which Henry VII rewarded him with £10 and a pension of £20 a year. Sebastian Cabot, his famous son, made further voyages until in 1509 he left England for Spain. While here he probably met Robert Thorne, a member of a wealthy Bristol merchant family who was especially interested in finding a north-west route to the

54 *The departure of John and Sebastian Cabot from Bristol on their first voyage of discovery of the New World of North America in 1497. Painting by Ernest Board, 1906.*

Indies. It was the navigational side of these voyages that excited Thorne's attention. He wrote a book setting out his ideas about a route to the East Indies over the Pole: the famous 'North-West Passage', which was to fascinate explorers for the next hundred years. In his book he includes a map of the world which, although small and in many ways amusingly crude, is on the whole surprisingly accurate. Among those who later searched for the North-West Passage was Thomas James of Bristol who left Bristol in 1631, hoping to have the good fortune to find the passage which would lead to the fabled wealth of India and Cathay.

At regular intervals throughout the 16th century, voyages of exploration continued; but the long years of war with Spain set back English colonisation. With the approach of peace, however, new ventures began. Richard Hakluyt, prebendary of Bristol and author of the *Famous Voyages*, took a great interest in the activities of the seaport. It was he and others who determined that Bristol should found a permanent English colony in America. Inspired by Hakluyt and financed by Bristol merchants, Martin Pring set sail from Bristol in 1603 with two ships, the *Speedwell* and *Discoverer*, 'for the further discovery of the north part of Virginia'. He anchored in a bay which he named Whitson Bay in honour of John Whitson, the chief promoter of the expedition; later to be called Plymouth Harbour.

Three years later Pring made a second voyage to New England mainly financed by Sir Ferdinando Gorges and Sir John Popham. This

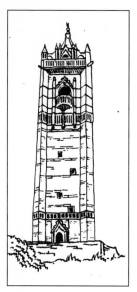

55 *Cabot Tower.*

resulted in the granting of the first colonial charter for the settlement of North Virginia. The New England pilgrims followed in his train and settled in a land already surveyed by Bristol merchants. New England, however, was not the only scene of Bristol's colonising activities. In 1610, John Guy of Bristol with John Slany of London and other merchants, foreseeing the great possibilities which lay in Cabot's Newfoundland, obtained a charter from James I enabling the 'Company of Adventurers and Planters of London and Bristol' to colonise these northern latitudes. With a band of settlers made up of fellow citizens, John Guy sailed out to found the colony of which he was made the first Governor. He also took with him 'hens, ducks, pigeons, cowes, goats, kine and other live creatures'. In the following years, a local chronicler records, 'Also this year Mr. Guy did carry to Newfoundland 10 heyfers, 2 bulls, 60 goats, and 16 women'.

Guy met with opposition from the fishermen who had settled there and were accustomed to regard the island as their own. They resented any form of authority. In 1613 Guy returned home to his busy life in Bristol while the little settlement struggled on. Two years later John Barker, Master of the Society of Merchant Venturers of Bristol, bought land at Harbour Grace and made a successful colony at Bristol Hope. Meanwhile Bristol's interest in the Newfoundland fisheries continued to grow. Each year ships sailed to Newfoundland to exchange their goods for fish, or to fish themselves. Some of these returned straight home while others proceeded with their cargoes of salted cod to the ports of Spain and Portugal where the fish was exchanged for wines. Bristol was famous then, as it is today, for its 'milk'.

Throughout the 17th century, ships filled with men, women and children set sail from Bristol harbour to settle in the new colonies. They were of all classes. Some were landed gentry ruined by the Civil War. Others were escaping from religious persecution and there were those leaving the country 'for the country's good'. A record survives of some ten thousand men and women, 'servants to foreign plantations', who in the short space of 22 years—from 1654 to 1676—were transferred from Bristol to Virginia, Maryland, Barbados and New England.

One Virginian enterprise was particularly associated with Gloucestershire, being colonised by three shiploads of some ninety men and a few women, mostly from the Berkeley and Winchcombe areas. The first 35 men sailed from Bristol in the little 47-ton ship *Margaret* in the autumn of 1619. After ten weeks they made landfall in the James River to establish the Berkeley Plantation, where they were joined by the rest of the party under two Gloucestershire squires, George Thorpe of Berkeley and William Tracy of Stanway, both of whom had been driven overseas by their debts at home. They attempted to establish the first foundry in the New World, but the little colony was struck by disease and the Indian uprising of Good Friday 1622. Within a few years only one-tenth of those who had sailed hopefully down the Severn still survived along the James River in Virginia. Such were the risks of colonial ventures.

11

Gloucestershire Schools

The oldest schools in Bristol and Gloucestershire were religious foundations. The King's School at Gloucester may claim a direct connection with the medieval choristers' school of St Peter's Abbey, and other abbeys also maintained schools. Some ancient schools were attached to chantries in parish churches, where the priest's duties included the teaching of children. One of the oldest and most remarkable of these was at Wotton-under-Edge, which has the distinction of being the earliest school founded by a lay person and the first founded by a woman. In 1384 Katherine Lady Berkeley built a house in Wotton for a master and two poor boys, modelling the statutes on those of Winchester, founded two years earlier.

When the chantries were abolished during the Reformation in 1547-8 the Chantry Commissioners recommended in vain that the Crown should establish new grammar schools. Fortunately wealthy Tudor and Stuart benefactors made good the deficiency caused by the Crown. At Cheltenham Richard Pate built a school in 1571 and at Newland Edward Bell about 1577, both being endowed with former chantry property.

56 *Bell's Grammar School, Newland. The original stone school-house built under the terms of the will of Edward Bell (d.1577) and used until the school was moved to Coleford in 1875.*

57 *Queen Elizabeth's Hospital schoolboy.*

58 *Red Maids' school-girl.*

Other new schools included the Crypt school at Gloucester (1540), Stow (*c*.1550) and Northleach (1559). At the beginning of the 17th century more new schools were founded at Tetbury (1610), Wickwar (1627) and Henbury (1631).

In the city of Bristol in the reign of Henry VII a grammar school had been attached to the abbey of St Augustine. When the abbey became the cathedral church in 1542 the school was refounded. During the 17th century the wealthy merchants spent their money in establishing new schools rather than by making gifts to the church. In 1532 Robert and Nicholas Thorne founded a grammar school 'for boys to be taught in good manners and literature'. John Carr, a soapboiler who died in 1586, was the founder of Queen Elizabeth's Hospital on the model of Christ's Hospital, London. All of these schools were for boys, but in 1634 John Whitson, very much ahead of his time, provided a boarding school for girls, which was known as the Red Maids' School from the colour of the girls' dresses.

All the boys' schools were 'grammar' schools where the master taught Latin and Greek grammar, languages and logic. The decorated foundation charter of Pate's grammar school at Cheltenham shows an Elizabethan classroom. The master stands at his desk where the small boys, sitting on a bench and sharing books, presented their exercises. There was no restriction on the fashionable excesses of Elizabethan dress, and a basket of balls stood awaiting the end of the lesson. In a corner there was a birch for punishment.

Half a century later the governors of Bell's grammar school at Newland laid down rules for the good behaviour of both master and boys. After they had passed an entrance test the master had to 'teach diligently all children who come to him ... according to their capacities'. He was to 'train them up in good manners' and take them regularly to church. The school hours were from 7 or 8 a.m. to 5 or 6 p.m. with a dinner break of two hours. Thursdays and Saturdays were half holidays, and there were six weeks' holidays at Christmas, Easter and Whitsun when 'some exercises are then to bee made by the Scholars according to their abilities'.

At the beginning of the 18th century Edward Colston, one of Bristol's most remarkable benefactors, founded and endowed a school where boys were to be taught writing, arithmetic and church catechism. This school flourishes today. In his parish of Temple, Colston also endowed another school for 'the educating in reading and writing, cyphering and perfecting in the church catechism as it is now established by law and also for the clothing of 44 boys of the parish, forever'. A visitor to the school in 1710 said 'it did my heart good to see and hear those fatherless and friendless children spell, read, write, respond to the catechism, say graces and prayers and several verses in scripture without book'. There were other charity schools founded by Bristol merchants during the 18th century.

In the county at this period all the older schools, with the exception of the King's School at Gloucester, were declining, and the initiative for founding new ones passed to the nonconformists. The Unitarian minister, James Forbes, ran an academy in Gloucester from 1696 to 1712, and a more famous one was established by one of his teachers, Samuel Jones, about 1708. At Kingswood George Whitefield and John Wesley founded schools in 1739 and 1746. The latter (moved to Bath in 1852) was a boarding school with a hard regime and fierce discipline. A few schools, for instance at Stroud and Wotton-under-Edge, were started by the Anglican Society for the Promotion of Christian Knowledge, one of whose founders in 1698 was Colonel Maynard Colchester of Westbury-on-Severn. The haphazard efforts of charity and dame schools, or the village curate, were possibly well summed up by the steward of the Foley estates at Newent in his account book for 1690. 'Paid a drunken Priest schooling (or rather deceiving) poor boyes 1 yeare, £1.' In 1815 a penurious and unskilled gentleman, a warehouseman, and a retired Army sergeant all thought themselves well qualified to apply for the mastership of Bisley Bluecoat school. There were many places, even as large as Uley, where there was no school at all.

At first the deficiency was partly filled by Sunday schools. One of the earliest appears to have been started in Nailsworth by the Independent minister, J.M. Moffatt, but a Gloucester parson, Thomas Stock, soon followed his example in 1780. Rob-

59 *Robert Raikes (1735-1811), owner of the* Gloucestershire Journal *and promoter of Sunday Schools.*

ert Raikes, then owner of the *Gloucester Journal*, extended Stock's activities and gave the Sunday schools much publicity in his newspaper. A few years later Andrew Bell, who lived at Cheltenham for a time, founded the National Society in 1811. Hundreds of church schools were started by the Society throughout the country, and where nonconformist traditions were strong British schools were established. The one at Tewkesbury was one of the first in 1812, and the first master of the British school at Wotton-under-Edge was Isaac Pitman, who wrote his *Stenographic Soundhand* while there. Later, under the Education Act 1870, school boards were set up to provide schools where there was a need, as at Kingswood, Oldland and Warmley, where children six years old were still working in the coal mines.

For those who could afford to pay for their education a number of

60 *Robert Raikes's first Sunday School, Gloucester.*

academies for ladies and gentlemen had long been established in Bristol. In 1758 Hannah More and her four sisters opened a Young Ladies' Academy in Park Street 'where French, reading, writing, arithmetic and needlework were carefully taught; and a dancing master attended'. George Pocock took pupils at four guineas a year. The advertisement for his Academy in 1795 ran as follows: 'My system of education is calculated chiefly for the men of business, and includes penmanship in all its hands, elocution, arithmetic, mensuration illustrated by globes, accompanied with a general view of the commercial world.' The Dursley Commercial school, founded about 1840, provided a similar practical education. The reform of the archaic constitutions and old-fashioned syllabuses of the grammar schools came too late to prevent the extension of private education. Cheltenham College (1841) was the first of the Victorian public schools. Clifton College followed in 1861. A more startling innovation was the serious education of girls, which owes much to the determination of Miss Dorothea Beale at Cheltenham Ladies' College (1853). In Bristol, Clifton High School (1877) and Redland High School (1882) similarly met the demand of the Victorian middle class for girls' education.

Few men achieved more in educational reform in Victorian times than the evangelical Rev. Francis Close of Cheltenham, later Dean of Carlisle. He was largely influential in the reform of Cheltenham Grammar School, aided the foundation of both the boys' and girls' public schools in the town, founded about a dozen National and infants' schools, and, most important of all, founded St Paul's and St Mary's teacher training colleges in 1847, so that he might no more be able to say that 'the commonest qualification for school teaching was failure at one's trade, especially tailoring or shoemaking'.

A generation later in Bristol another cleric, Prebendary John Percival, then headmaster of Clifton College, was advocating another advance in education, the foundation of local universities. Endowed through the generosity of the Wills family, the University College, Bristol, was opened in 1876. A further stage was achieved in 1909 when the University received its charter which provided for the incorporation of the University College, the Merchant Venturers' Technical College (1856) and the Bristol Medical School (1833).

12

Gloucestershire Houses

Gloucestershire is well endowed with the natural building materials of timber, stone and clay. Apart from churches, castles and a few other outstanding buildings, stone was little used before Tudor times, and timber provided the usual framework for most houses not only in the Vale, where it continued in use until about 1750, but also in the Forest of Dean and the Cotswolds.

Probably the oldest inhabited home in the county is Berkeley Castle, still lived in by the Berkeley family for whom Henry II built the oldest surviving part, the great stone keep, in 1153-6. This keep, which stands on the mound of the first castle raised immediately after the Norman Conquest by William FitzOsbern, contains a great hall and chapel, and in one corner is the dungeon where Edward II was imprisoned and murdered in 1327. Long before then, Maurice Lord Berkeley (1171-90) had built a new hall within the curtain wall of the castle, and Thomas Berkeley (1325-61) rebuilt this hall and a new chapel adjoining it, which has texts written on its beams taken from the translation of the Bible by John Trevisa, chaplain to the Berkeleys from about 1385 to 1402. For much of the 15th and early 16th centuries the ownership of the castle was in dispute. The claim of the Warwick family was irrevocably destroyed with the defeat and death of Lord Lisle at the battle of Nibley Green in 1470, the last private feudal conflict on English soil. Two centuries later there was warfare again at the castle, when in 1645 it was the last Royalist stronghold in Gloucestershire to surrender during the Civil War. Its Norman outer bailey was razed and the keep wall breached to prevent the castle being used again for military purposes.

The crudest form of timber-framing was the simple cruck construction found throughout the west Midlands and Welsh Marches. In Gloucestershire there are well-known examples at Deerhurst,

61 *Tewkesbury. The Norman tower of the abbey church dominates the riverside town with its many timber box-framed and jettied houses.*

62 *Stanton. Pre-inclosure stone farm-houses with typical Cots-wold architectural fea-tures of stone slate roofs, steep gables, dormers, mullioned windows and dripmoulds line the vil-lage street.*

Didbrook and Dymock, but recently many more have been discovered (though much altered) in the Vale south of Gloucester. Most of them were built in the 15th and 16th centuries. Wealthy townsmen imitated fashions spreading from London and the south-east for timber-framed buildings with walls of vertical stud beams set close together, the upper floors jettied or overhanging downstairs, and late in the 16th century the fashion, particularly for jettied houses, spread among the richer squires and yeomen farmers. Their increasing wealth in late Elizabethan times coincided with a growing shortage of good timber so that constructional methods more economical of wood were introduced. Throughout the whole of the Vale are hundreds of box-framed farmhouses and cottages built between about 1600 and 1750.

Few medieval town houses survive. At Gloucester the *New Inn* was built about 1450 by John Twyning, a monk of Gloucester Abbey, where up to 200 merchants, pilgrims and travellers might stay. Shops fronted the street and within its courtyards were several parlours and private dining rooms, a communal hall for servants, kitchens and stables. The two upper storeys had more than forty rooms for guests. Unlike private houses of the period, which still lacked passages, the inn rooms were approached by galleries to preserve the privacy and possessions of the guests. In Tewkesbury merchants' houses at that time had workshops downstairs with a shop facing the street, and an entrance at one side of the house. The main living-room was on the first floor. Smaller houses had the main living-room behind the shop, heated by an open hearth, with a single room over the shop. There is a unique terrace of such houses built about 1500 adjoining the abbey graveyard. The town was

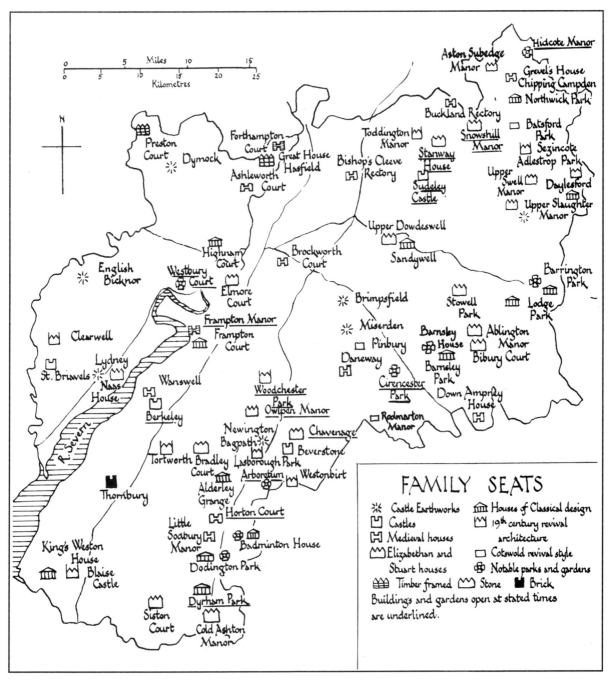

FAMILY SEATS

✳ Castle Earthworks   ⬜ Houses of Classical design
⬜ Castles   ⬗ 19th century revival architecture
⬜ Medieval houses
⬜ Elizabethan and Stuart houses   ⬜ Cotswold revival style
⬜ Timber framed   ⬜ Stone   ⬛ Brick
⬗ Notable parks and gardens
Buildings and gardens open at stated times are underlined.

confined by flood meadows and, as it grew in population from about 1700, cottages were built along the long backyards of the older houses, approached by the side entrances and alleyways which became a distinctive feature of the town; many were demolished as slums in the 20th century.

63 *Family seats.*

64 *Cotswold stone house, Chipping Camden.*

In the Cotswolds timber-framing was also used until the shortage of wood in the 16th century, and old framed houses have been discovered, for instance, at Painswick and Stroud concealed beneath later stonework. Archaeologists have proved that 13th- and 14th-century cottages at Blockley were stone built, but in most places the first stone buildings date from about 1550, and nearly all surviving Cotswold stone houses date from Elizabeth I's reign or later. The oldest stone houses in the Forest of Dean follow the fashions set in the Cotswolds. The chief features are steeply pitched and gabled roofs of stone slates, small mullioned windows and doors with dripmoulds, and the style lingered long because of the conservatism of masons and the remoteness of the wold villages. The builders of Cotswold farmhouses made only cautious concessions to changing ideas, unlike the bolder contemporary designs of the great architects like Samuel Hauduroy and William Talman at Dyrham Park (1692-1702), Sir John Vanbrugh at Kings Weston House (1711-14), William Kent at Badminton (1740 alterations) and James Wyatt at Dodington Park (1796-1813). The traditional style was revived late in the 19th century by architects of the Arts and Crafts Movement, such as Ernest Gimson and Ernest and Sidney Barnsley, who all arrived in 1893, Guy Dawber and Norman Jewson, with the result that modern building on the Cotswolds has been perhaps unduly trammelled.

Brick is a more versatile material than either timber or stone, and it has been extensively used in the Vale since the beginning of the 17th century. At first it was used only for chimneys. An unusually early example of brick building is Thornbury Castle, built for Edward Duke of Buckingham in 1510-21. John Clifford rebuilt Frampton Court in brick in 1650-1 (demolished 1731) dug from local clay pits. At about the same time there were brick works near Gloucester. In 1752 one firing only of a brick clamp in north-west Gloucestershire produced 58,000 bricks at 5s. a thousand and 18,000 tiles at 8s. a thousand. Although fine 18th-century brick houses survive, designed in the symmetrical mode dictated by Renaissance styles, fashionably inclined architects determined that a

65 *Dyrham Park. The west range designed for Secretary William Blathwayt by Samuel Hauduroy in 1692 is more delicate than the east range of 1698-1704 by William Talman, Comptroller of Royal Works.*

IV *Mayor-making ceremony at Bristol, illustrated in the Mayor's Calendar compiled by Robert Ricart, Town Clerk, in 1499.*

V *The Lord Mayor's Chapel at College Green, Bristol is the only privately-owned civic church in England. It was bought by the City at the Dissolution in 1541 for use as a chapel for the Lord Mayor and Corporation.*

VI *Temple Guiting. A timeless Cotswold winter scene with sheep grazing around the church.*

VII *Cirencester church, the largest parish church in Gloucestershire, was extensively rebuilt by wealthy wool merchants in the 15th and early 16th centuries.*

66 *Badminton House. The first Duke of Beaufort built the house at the end of the 17th century. The flanking pavilions and the cupolas designed by William Kent were added by c.1740.*

good house should at least appear to be built of stone. The builders of Georgian and early Victorian Cheltenham raised houses of noble proportions and attractive details, but their elegant appearance of stone or stucco hides the constructional brickwork.

Great households were run by an army of servants. At Badminton in 1836 there was a staff of 272 in the house and on the estate, a complete village in itself. Every week two beasts and 16 sheep were slaughtered for consumption in the house. The stables contained 119 horses and there were 90 couples of hounds of the Beaufort Hunt in the kennels. When the hunt met at Badminton the eighth Duke of Beaufort (1824-99) entertained up to a thousand followers for breakfast. A generation earlier William Cother, an elderly gentleman, mayor of Gloucester in 1836 and living alone just outside the city, had two servants and a gardener. He took a new cook in 1837 at nine guineas [£9.45] a year and she was instructed to 'obey orders without grumbling, cut and leave meat fit to come to table when cold, make no waste, leave no fat, use economy on all occasions, ask leave whenever she goes from home, never leave the house after night', and she was allowed one day off a month. William Cother was a keen gardener who owned a mowing machine, perhaps one of those developed from cloth shearing machines in 1830 by Edwin Budding of Stroud. In his time the great landscaped parks of 'Capability' Brown at Badminton and Dodington and Charles Harcourt Masters and Humphry Repton at Dyrham were in their prime, but an older formal Dutch water garden created by Maynard Colchester at Westbury-on-Severn between 1697 and 1706 may still be seen. His purchases of plants included 3,500 yew and holly trees, 300 fruit trees, 2,000 asparagus crowns and 600 bulbs.

13

The Civil War

67 *Civil War standards, Bromsberrow.*

The religious and political tensions which erupted in the Civil War had their origins in the Reformation and social and economic changes of Tudor reigns. The Puritans grew in numbers and influence especially in Bristol and Gloucester and many early 17th-century town clergy had Puritan leanings. At Deerhurst the communion table still has the seats around it which were placed there in Puritan fashion before 1606, and William Laud, when Dean of Gloucester, offended both bishop Miles Smith and the citizens by ordering in 1617 'that the communion table should be placed altarwise at the upper end of the quire close to the east wall' of the cathedral.

Charles I's autocratic government without Parliament and his grants of monopolies were also unpopular. Both the county members of Parliament, Nathaniel Stephens and John Dutton, went to prison rather than pay Ship Money. Gloucestershire tobacco growers defied the Virginian monopoly, and commoners vigorously complained of Sir John Wynter's grant of the Forest of Dean when he started inclosure and felling. Nevertheless when war did break out the county gentry mostly supported the king, and the castles of Berkeley and Sudeley were garrisoned. On the other hand, John Dutton, M.P., somewhat unwillingly followed Charles to Oxford under the threat of having his house burnt down. Later he became friendly with Cromwell, who wrote that he 'hath given so many real testimonies of his affection to the Government and to my person in particular ... that no man I know in England hath done more'.

Bristol, like most of the larger towns, sided with Parliament and, as the key to the West, played an important part in the war. None of the great battles was fought in Gloucestershire but the Royalist attacks on Bristol and Gloucester in 1643 have been interpreted as the turning point in the war. As both parties knew, whoever controlled Bristol must in the end control the West.

After the battle of Edgehill some effort was made to strengthen Bristol against attack, but this was not easy as the town lay in a hollow and the medieval walls were useless. A series of earthworks was erected on the northern side of the city whilst the walls on the southern side were strengthened. The Parliamentary forces in the town were under the command of Colonel Fiennes, son of Lord Saye and Sele. On 26 July 1643

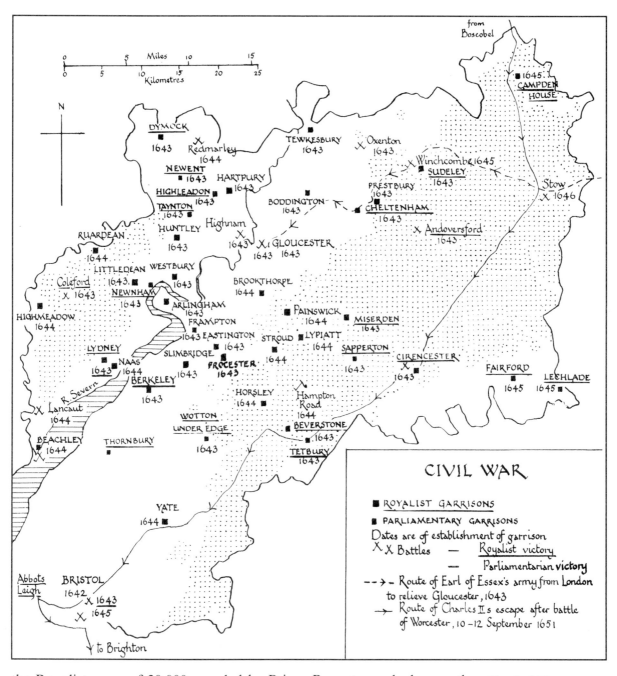

the Royalist army of 20,000 men led by Prince Rupert marched upon the **68** *Civil War.*
town from Cirencester, making their way through Westbury-on-Trym to
Clifton. After severe fighting, Fiennes agreed to a truce and a treaty of
peace was signed.

The king now had the choice of marching on London at once or
delaying to secure his rear by winning Gloucester, where although the

69 *Edward Massey.*

city walls had been repaired there was only a small and isolated garrison of 1,500 men. On 10 August he called on them to obey him and open the city, but reckoned without the spirit of alderman Thomas Pury, Edward Massey, the young commander of the garrison, and other leading citizens, who replied,

> We do keep this city according to our oaths and allegiance, to and for the use of his Majesty and his royal posterity: and do accordingly conceive ourselves wholly bound to obey the commands of his Majesty, signified by both Houses of Parliament: and are resolved by God's help to keep this city accordingly.

After a fortnight of mining and tunnelling, raids and counter attacks the city was still not taken. In London the significance of the siege was appreciated, and on 26 August the Earl of Essex with 8,000 men left the capital to relieve Gloucester. Marching over the Cotswolds, and through Prestbury and Cheltenham, the weary and rain-soaked Londoners fired signals to hearten the besieged. After almost a month on 4 September the Royalists started to withdraw, ignorant that Gloucester was down to its last three barrels of gunpowder. As the besiegers pulled back to Painswick the royal princes are said to have asked their father when they were going home. Disconsolately the king replied that 'he had no home to go to'.

Between then and September 1645 there followed a restless interval during which the Royalist cause went from bad to worse. In Gloucestershire Massey enlarged the range of his successful raids from Gloucester, wiping out the isolated Royalist strongholds, and after the Parliamentary victory at Naseby (Northants.) on 14 June the situation looked black and ominous for the king.

Bristol remained in Royalist hands and Prince Rupert, hearing that the onslaught was about to begin, ordered the villages around the city to be burned. Westbury, Clifton and Bedminster were fired. The plight of the people within the city was dire. Plague had broken out and one hundred persons were dying every week. Three thousand are said to have perished. The advance on the city was made by way of Hanham, and tradition places the holding of a council of war between General Fairfax and Oliver Cromwell at Wickham Court. The storming of the city took place according to plan and the city surrendered. On 17 September 1645 the House of Commons ordered a national thanksgiving for its capture, and ten years later the castle was destroyed by order of Cromwell. The last battle of the war was at Stow-on-the-Wold on 21 March 1646 when Lord Astley, the defeated Royalist general, captured and sitting on a drum, said prophetically, 'Ye may now sit and play, for you have done all your worke if you fall not out among yourselves'.

This was what happened. Oliver Cromwell with the support of the army subdued Parliament with its majority of Presbyterian members, but was then faced with the wrath of the Scots, angered further by the execution of Charles Stuart. The country remained unquiet despite the

70 *Sudeley Castle, 1732, in ruins after the Civil War. It was restored by the Dent family who bought it in 1837.*

strength of Cromwell's position and the punishment of Royalist supporters, whose power was weakened by heavy fines and the loss of their property. The estates of the Earl of Worcester, ancestor of the Dukes of Beaufort, were confiscated and handed over to Cromwell himself, Berkeley and Sudeley castles were slighted, while lesser men like Thomas Chamberlayne of Stow faced their persecutors with pleas of the losses that they had already suffered from both sides seeking billets and supplies.

It is not surprising that Royalist sympathies remained warm, if discreetly hidden. Charles II after his defeat at Worcester in 1651 rode undetected through Gloucestershire on his way to Abbots Leigh outside Bristol, where his friends hoped to charter a ship to take him to France and on Cromwell's death plots for his restoration multiplied. In 1659 Massey, who had changed sides and been in exile with Charles II returned secretly to lead a rising in Gloucestershire, but was arrested at Wotton-under-Edge. He escaped, and after Charles II's successful restoration the next year he was elected member of Parliament for Gloucester. The wheel of fortune had turned the full circle. The king, who as a boy of 13 had witnessed the city's defiance of his father, ordered its walls to be levelled and deprived it of the in-shire territory.

14

Tobacco, Sugar and Slaves

The part Bristol played in the colonisation of the New World helped her to expand her trade and to develop new and valuable industries. At first tobacco was only imported into London but this led to so much smuggling in the Bristol Channel that in 1639 the trade was thrown open and tobacco was allowed to be brought into Bristol and other ports. Once established in Bristol the tobacco trade flourished. In 1666, out of a convoy of 23 ships that arrived at Bristol, 19 were laden with tobacco from Virginia and Barbados. Although laws had long been in force prohibiting the growing of tobacco in England, large quantities continued to be grown, especially in Gloucestershire. Many attempts to destroy the plantations were made by the Government, often resulting in riots. It is not surprising that the Bristol merchants vigorously opposed the growing of tobacco in Gloucestershire. M. Jorevin de Rochefort, Treasurer of France, on a visit to Bristol noticed the prevalence of tobacco smoking.

71 *The head of the Quay, Bristol, showing St Stephen's tower on the left and Bristol Cathedral in the background, 1826.*

'Supper being finished,' he says 'they set on the table half a dozen pipes and a packet of Tobacco for smoking, which is a general custom amongst women, as well as men, who think that without Tobacco one cannot live in England because they say it dissipates the humours of the brain.'

The manufacture of ordinary clay pipes began in Bristol at an early date. The bowls were at first little longer than a thimble, for the price of tobacco was very high. In the markets, it was sold for its weight in silver. Smoking became popular. The members of the Corporation were also ardent smokers, but economical, sending their foul pipes back to the kiln to be purified by burning. The Chamberlain of Bristol paid for 'one gross of pipes and for burning of foul pipes, 2s.'.

Having created a desire for sugar in preference to honey amongst the more wealthy, Bristol merchants sought ways to extend this trade, and Robert Aldworth in 1612 set up the plant for the first sugar refinery in England. Such was the popularity of sugar that when the Corporation made gifts to those who might be described as friends at court, sugar was always a substantial part of the gift. The Earl of Pembroke, Lord High Steward of the city, received among other delicacies a half hundred-weight of loaf sugar at 20d. [8p] per pound. On another occasion when the Recorder brought his wife to Bristol, the lady had a present of sugar loaves, comfits and prunes. The great demand for sugar as one of the necessities of life made Bristol the chief sugar-refining town in the country. There were no less than twenty sugar refineries along the banks of the Rivers Avon and Frome. John Evelyn recounts his visit to one of them in 1654. 'Here,' he says, 'I first saw the manner of refining sugar and casting it into loaves where we had a collation of eggs fried in the sugar furnace together with excellent spanish wine.' Very lively and picturesque the Bristol quays must have been in the days of the refineries, for whole flotillas of West Indian traders were frequently in the port together.

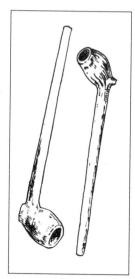

72 *Clay tobacco pipes.*

When shiploads of transported prisoners and indentured servants failed to meet the growing demand for cheap labour on the tobacco and sugar plantations, England turned to Africa for slaves. By the end of the 17th century Bristol was one of the most active centres of the slave trade in England. The outward voyage of a slave trader was made with a cargo of trinkets, beads, hardware, pottery and firearms, which were exchanged for slaves off the coast of West Africa. These slaves were sold on arrival at the plantations, largely in the West Indies, at their market value, and sugar, molasses, tobacco and rum were brought back to Bristol. Upon this traffic and the ancillary trades that grew with it— the building and fitting out of ships, the manufacture of many articles of tin, iron, copper, brass and clothing—Bristol depended for its prosperity for more than one hundred years. The heyday of slaving was during the period 1660 to 1786, when Thomas Clarkson began his campaign for its abolition. In 1725, Bristol ships carried 16,950 slaves to the plantations. In 1755, of the 473 members of the African Company 237 resided in Bristol. It is said that out of every hundred slaves shipped only about half survived the voyage: it was a lucrative but inhuman trade. That the

73 *Shackles from a slave ship.*

74 *Anti-slave-trade medallion.*

movement for the abolition of slavery made early headway in Bristol is perhaps surprising. Among the first to take united action against it were the Quakers, who were an influential body in Bristol. They were strengthened by the vigorous support of John Wesley. The slave trade was abolished in 1807, the movement for emancipation followed shortly; and in 1833 the slaves were freed.

During the 18th century Bristol was engaged in another kind of lucrative trade: privateering. It was not by chance that Robert Louis Stevenson in his *Treasure Island* chose Bristol as the port from which his gang of pirates should set out, for Bristol was a haunt of pirates and privateers. Between piracy and privateering there was only a sheet of paper—the letter of marque. Ships were constantly slipping out of the Avon filled with men who were past masters at this rough and ready sea game. Privateering ships were furnished by Bristol merchants whose wealth was greatly increased by this form of speculation. One of the most famous of these expeditions, that of the *Duke* and *Duchess*, two ships under the command of Captain Woodes Rogers, Thomas Dover and William Dampier, was not only a financial success, but it gave to the world that great classic—*Robinson Crusoe*.

15

The Forest of Dean

In both its topography and history the land between the Severn and the Wye is a distinctive region of Gloucestershire. Much of the area lay within the Forest of Dean. The term 'forest' is a legal one meaning an area reserved by the Crown for hunting with special laws for the protection of the game and their covert. The Forest of Dean was afforested soon after the Norman Conquest, and the Norman kings imposed an efficient administration. At St Briavels, a castle was built *c*.1131 by Miles, Earl of Hereford, as the seat of the Constable of the Forest. The boundaries of the Forest were defined from the mouth of the Wye to Over bridge outside Gloucester, up the Leadon valley to Newent, and westwards along the county boundary to the Wye near Monmouth. In the late 13th century these limits were reduced to the present-day extent. (See map, p.74.)

Both William I and John hunted in the Forest, but the royal preserves were also constantly attacked by wolves and poachers, who included in the 13th century such important men as Roger Bigod, Earl

75 *St Briavels Castle.*

76 *Speech House. Since 1676 the Verderers of the Forest have met in the court room at the King's Lodge or Speech House, now a hotel.*

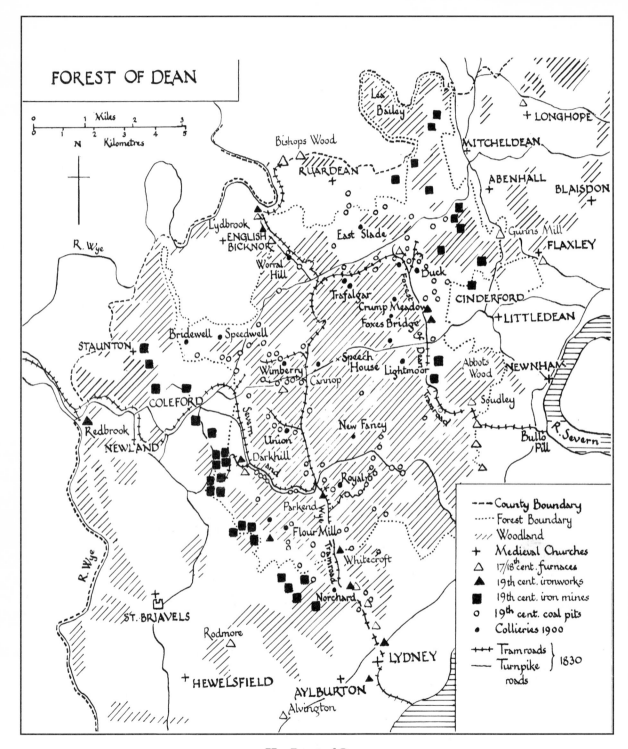

77   *Forest of Dean.*

of Norfolk, and the abbot of Tintern. The value of the hunting declined from the 16th century, but the importance of the woodland increased with the demands of local industry and naval shipbuilders. The diarist John Evelyn in 1663 believed 'that in the great Expedition of 1588, it was expressly enjoined the Spanish Commanders of that signal Armada, that if when landed they should not be able to subdue our Nation, they should yet be sure not to leave a tree standing in the Forest of Dean'. Despite this the English government did little to preserve Dean timber until the importance of a navy was emphasised by the 17th-century Dutch wars of Evelyn's own time.

By then the value of the Forest, particularly Lea Bailey, as a source of navy timber was fully appreciated. Samuel Pepys, Secretary to the Navy, visited the Forest in 1671 and was disappointed to find 'little encouragement to expect much thence for the support of the Navy in future ages'. One of the difficulties was transport within the Forest and the distance from shipyards, although ships were built at Bristol, Lydney and Newnham. Despite Pepys's forebodings the Forest continued to supply great quantities of naval timber, including 30,000 loads between 1761 and 1802, which caused Nelson in his turn to report that 'The state of the Forest at this moment is deplorable, for if my information is true, there is not 3,500 loads of timber in the whole Forest fit for [ship] building'. Nelson was perhaps exaggerating, but only the planting and good management of Edward Machen, the Deputy Surveyor from 1808 to 1854, enabled the Forest to supply good timber for the nation during the two 20th-century World Wars.

The woodland was also a supply of charcoal for the iron furnaces and forges. From at least Roman times iron ore was obtained from the

78   *Freeminer.*

Forest. In 1086 Gloucester paid to the Crown a rent of 36 loads and 100 rods of iron from the Forest, and by the late 13th century there were between 40 and 60 forges at work producing an average of about 150 tons of iron a year, about one sixth of the country's production. By the early 14th century the traditional rights of the inhabitants of the parishes bordering the Forest to dig for iron ore, coal or stone had been set down in writing, and from the 17th century the freeminers' Mine Law Court was meeting regularly to settle disputes. Mines or 'gales' were claimed and registered with the chief official of the court, the Gaveller. A freeminer is defined as a man born and living within the

79   *Hopewell Mine. A typical small free mine which closed in 1993. The freeminer continues to work a nearby mine which has connecting levels with Hopewell.*

hundred of St Briavels (which includes the Forest of Dean) who has worked there a year and a day in a coal or iron mine.

Ancient methods of smelting and forging persisted in the Forest until the early 17th century but, by 1640 11 blast furnaces and 11 forges were probably the greatest concentration of ironworks in the country. In 1613 alone about 1,400 tons of ore were exported to Ireland. With little regard for the customs of the free miners and commoners, thereby provoking riots, the rival ironmasters struggled for greater concessions from the Crown. Sir John Wynter of Lydney was the most successful. In 1640 he virtually bought the whole Forest for £106,000 and an annual rent of £1,950 and immediately started felling and inclosure. He aroused such local opposition that his grant was withdrawn.

For much of the 18th century iron production was largely in the hands of the Foley partnership. Paul Foley, a Black Country iron-master, purchased the king's works in the Forest in 1674. By 1717 he had expanded his production and had six blast furnaces, which made three-quarters of the 5,000 tons of pig iron coming from the area. Most was shipped from Newnham and Ashleworth to the Black Country forges, but other people's wireworks in the Wye valley sent their goods to Bristol.

Because of the abundant local supply of charcoal the Forest iron-masters were slow to introduce coke for iron smelting, and it was not until 1795 that the first coke-fired furnaces were built at Cinderford Ironworks. By 1841 the works made 12,000 tons of iron annually, its size, energetic management under the Crawshay family, and good rail communications enabling it to survive until 1894, the last of the Forest ironworks. The 19th-century hillside town of Cinderford owes its existence to the works. At the peak of production in 1871 the annual output of ore from the Forest was almost 200,000 tons, but conservative methods, inaccessibility, and inventions that overcame the difficulty of using low grade ore from other ironfields, all contributed to the failure of the Forest works. The difficulties experienced by Sir Henry Bessemer in making steel from low grade ore were overcome by Robert Forester Mushet, who invented a new process at Darkhill in 1856. Earlier his father David Mushet of Coleford had built the Darkhill furnace in 1818-19 where he succeeded in making a superior refined iron.

The decline in the iron industry in the late 19th century was balanced by the increase in coal mining. The free miners had dug coal since the Middle Ages, and Coleford was already so named in 1282. In the late 17th century production was sufficient for the Mine Law Court

80 *Shakemantle Iron Mine, Ruspidge near Cinderford. The mine was sunk about 1830 and by 1841 belonged to the Crawshay family, Welsh iron and coal masters.*

81 *Trafalgar Colliery, Cinderford, c.1900. It worked a thin but high quality coal seam from the 1840s to about 1925. In 1882 it became the first colliery in the world to use electricity below the ground for motive power.*

to issue regulations about measures and prices, which in 1701 were not to exceed 5s. [25p] a ton to the inhabitants of the Forest or less than 6s. [30p] a ton to outsiders. Prices at the pithead were still less than 5s. [25p] a ton in 1788 when there were some 90 small pits producing about 100,000 tons a year. The pits were shallow, few being more than 25 feet deep owing to their liability to flooding.

By 1856 there were 221 mines producing about 600,000 tons of coal and the peak was reached in the present century when the annual output was just over 1,300,000 tons in 1938. Decline was equally rapid owing to the small size of the collieries, the depth of the good coal, and the trouble with flooding. Large-scale production ceased entirely in 1965, but a few gales are still worked by free miners, whose rights were preserved at nationalisation in 1947. The industrial expansion was accompanied by a large growth of population, the newcomers raising squatters' cottages in the clearings of the woods.

Transport played an important part in the commercial development of the Forest, but until the late 18th century road communications were poor. There was, however, a regular maritime trade from the ports and landing places on the Severn and Wye with Bristol. The Forest supplied the city with coal, timber for ship- and house-building, bark for its tanneries, slag for its glassworks, and stone for its buildings. Well-known Bristol merchants like John Whitson (d. 1627), Henry (d. 1592) and James (d. 1678) Gough, and Thomas James (d. 1618) came from Forest families, and by their wills founded charities and schools in their birthplaces.

16

Gloucestershire Farmers

82 *Dixton, c.1730. Part of a haymaking scene looking towards Gretton, showing some of the many workers, men and women, needed to mow, rake, turn, stack and bring in the hay.*

The dissolution of the monasteries and subsequent sales of their lands introduced a new class of landowners to the county, shrewd merchants or high ranking officials like Sir Thomas Chamberlayne of Prestbury, a former ambassador whose son Thomas established the family estate near Stow-on-the-Wold in 1602, William Whitmore of London who bought Lower Slaughter in 1611, or Richard Master, Physician to Elizabeth I who was granted the Cirencester Abbey estate in 1564. Most of the

really large estates were in the south of the county like Berkeley, Badminton, Cirencester Park or Tortworth, but locally powerful squires lived in many Cotswold villages. By contrast in the Vale of Tewkesbury and west of the Severn there were fewer large landowners, and yeoman farmers had more opportunity to improve themselves, like the Holder family of Taynton who rose from labourers to squires in the course of the 17th century.

The new landowners were keenly interested in their property and quick to try innovations. One of the most unusual was tobacco growing which was introduced in the Winchcombe area in 1622 by John Stratford, a London merchant of Gloucestershire origin. In a few years he amassed £20,000 from his venture and cultivation spread in both the north of the county and near Bristol. Though laborious it was so important to the cottagers and small-holders of Winchcombe and Cheltenham that they defied troops sent in 1658 and 1667 to destroy the crops that deprived Virginia of its monopoly.

83 *Farmhouse at Shepperdine, with cheese chamber under the roof. The shuttered window would be opened to ventilate the stacked cheeses.*

Poor cottagers also benefited from the cider trade which became a speciality of north-west Gloucestershire from about 1600. 'About Dymock ... the whole country may be said to be a forest of fruit trees,' wrote William Marshall in 1789, when the growers of the west Midland counties, after 'supplying their own immoderate consumption', sold more than a million and a half gallons for the London and Bristol markets. Even a labourer might earn £15 to £20 from his few fruit trees at a time when his whole year's wages amounted to a similar sum.

The farmers of the heavy lands of the Vale concentrated on dairying, and their farm houses from the late 16th century were equipped with cheese chambers for maturing and storing cheeses. The Double Gloucester, so called because it was made from a mixture of both the morning's and evening's milk, required a maturing period of several weeks. Production was at its peak in the century and a half from about 1700, and Marshall reckoned in 1789 that up to 1,200 tons were made in the Vale, chiefly from the Berkeley area.

The Cotswolds were then a far from attractive farming region. The thin stony soil produced light and weedy crops, and a landscape and houses that William Cobbett found so ugly in 1826 that he commented, 'this is a sort of country having less to please the eye than any other that I have ever seen'. Up to the end of the 18th century sheep 'still remain the grand object of the Cotswold husbandry' not only for wool, which

84 *Cider mill.*

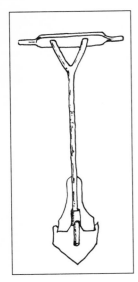

became coarser with cross-breeding, but also for meat. Many were sold to graziers in the Home Counties for fattening and slaughter and, like the Welsh cattle bought at Gloucester market, were taken along the drove roads over the wolds to the rich Thames Valley meadows on their way to Smithfield.

Improvements in arable farming were hampered by the continuance of the medieval open field system in which crop rotation was restricted and improvement of individual holdings impossible. The customary peasant land tenure of copyhold was progressively converted into shorter-term and more flexible leaseholds. West of the Severn many open fields were inclosed from the later Middle Ages to the 17th century, and on the Cotswolds there was also much inclosure in the 17th century. The large landowner benefited most by increased production. At Aldsworth, inclosed in 1793, the livestock was increased from 10 cattle and 200 sheep to 20 cattle and 1,800 sheep, and grain yield from 720 quarters to 2,360 quarters.

85 *Cotswold breast-plough.*

Until the 18th century inclosure was usually carried out by private agreements, but thereafter it was more common for the principal landowners to obtain a private Act of Parliament. At Aston Blank most of the village had been acquired on his marriage in 1767 by the archbishop of Armagh. In 1794 he settled the estate on his Irish son-in-law, reserving for himself an annuity as great as the rents from the estate. His son-in-law, the Rev. M.H. Noble, therefore decided to inclose the farms so that he could raise the rents on the grounds that the farms were improved. An Inclosure Act was passed in 1795 and in the following eight months

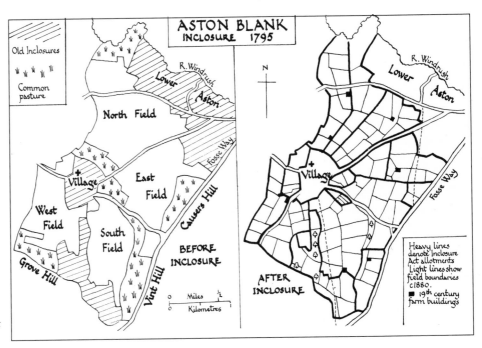

86 *Aston   Blank Inclosure, 1795.*

VIII *These Painswick houses bear many features of traditional Cotswold building—gabled and stone-slated roofs, mullioned windows, drip moulds and string-courses.*

IX *Dodington Park was designed for Christopher Bethell Codrington by James Wyatt between 1796 and 1812, set in the parkland landscaped a generation earlier by 'Capability' Brown.*

X *Stoke Orchard's open fields, mapped in 1751. The colours differentiate the scattered strips farmed by the principal landholders.*

87 *Aston Blank (now officially named Cold Aston). Windrush Farm, an isolated post-inclosure farm carved out of the former North Field after 1795.*

the three inclosure commissioners surveyed and re-allotted the village lands. The legal and fencing costs amounted to £1,915, or about £1.35 an acre, and the individual farmers were still faced with the cost of fencing their new farms with stone walls or hedges. Perhaps this was why they were behindhand with their rent, for it was these costs which affected the poorer tenants most seriously. At Cowley, although there was no depopulation, the small farmer disappeared entirely in the generations following inclosure in 1739. Before then there had been only one large farmer with 143 acres, 10 medium-sized holdings and 14 small holdings. By 1828 four men farmed 1,500 acres, there were four smallholders and 24 landless cottagers.

The small farmers, though inefficient, were right to fear inclosure for the loss of their independence. Even more unpopular was the inclosure of commons. At Bisley the weavers, who grazed their beasts and donkeys on the commons, successfully resisted inclosure in 1733. In 1847, however, these commons were inclosed despite the weavers' complaints, one angry anonymous writer demanding that the vicar, Rev. Thomas Keble, should support them, 'or, by God, I will shoot you'.

Inclosure was mostly completed by the mid-19th century, except in parts of the Vale, where the last Act was for inclosing the open fields of Elmstone Hardwicke in 1918. Other agricultural improvements followed. More diverse crop rotation was practised, steam ploughs were introduced from the 1860s, most successfully on the Cotswolds, and in the Vale Henry Clifford of Frampton-on-Severn was one landowner who drained the heavy clay lands, bought imported fertilisers, and bred better livestock. The Earls of Ducie were notable Gloucestershire reformers, who ran an experimental farm at Falfield in the 1840s, and built up a famous pedigree cattle herd. Farmers' clubs at Cirencester in 1828 and Westbury-on-Severn in 1840 were among the first, and even more sig-

88 *Stow Fair, c.1910 when the horse was still supreme. It remains one of the few great horse fairs in England.*

nificant was the establishment of the Agricultural College at Cirencester in 1845, and the first Young Farmers' Club at Berkeley in 1898.

In the late 19th century farming prosperity declined. The disastrous harvests of 1879 and following years, as well as overseas competition, had the long term effect of low rents and badly kept farms. One estate agent recalled that 'At that time [1890] it was exceedingly difficult to let farms at all and, consequently, people were afraid to do anything to upset the sitting tenant'. Labourers, who in 1830 had rioted around Tetbury and Fairford on the introduction of threshing machinery in fear of being unemployed, now voluntarily left the land in large numbers, and for the first time the population of remote villages declined.

17

The Cloth Industry

Gloucestershire clothiers manufactured almost exclusively a superfine broadcloth that was in great demand up to the mid-19th century. Its special characteristic of a smooth even surface like a billiard table cloth or a hunting jacket required a short, fine wool, and a good supply of water for fulling the cloth. This was one of the additional finishing processes which distinguished West Country broadcloths from the coarser worsteds produced more cheaply in the north of England.

By 1600 the industry was widely dispersed, and although there was a concentration of mills along the fast flowing rivers of the southern Cotswolds, particularly the Stroudwater, cloth was made at Berkeley and Thornbury, Newent and Lydbrook. A century later manufacture was almost entirely limited to the Stroud, Dursley and Wotton-under-Edge area, and the lower Stroudwater valley alone was producing 30,000 cloths a year.

The Gloucestershire clothiers did not then operate a factory system. The clothiers provided the capital for the purchase of the wool, and in their mills the woven cloth went through the various finishing processes but spinning and weaving were domestic industries. Most clothiers had

89 *A clothier from Avening with his pack ponies, 1791.*

only a small business, but even early in the 18th century Daniel Defoe commented that some were worth £40,000. Such gentlemen clothiers included Sir Onesiphorus Paul of Woodchester in the 18th century and Edward Sheppard of Gatcombe Park in the early 19th century. They had many dependents, for even an average clothier might provide work for 30 to 40 looms, and George Austin of Wotton-under-Edge claimed that he employed 200 to 300 men. A few like Paul Wathen of Lypiatt Park or Philip Sheppard squandered their fortunes, but those who failed were mostly smaller men with insufficient capital to survive

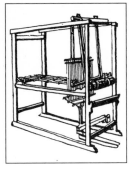

90 *Handloom.*

the recurring crises that affected the industry. In 1768 Daniel Packer of Painswick wrote, 'We shall have fewer Clothiers another year. I hear there was one sent to Gloster Jail Thursday last. And last Tuesday Sam. Haines (Brother to Mr. Daniel Haines) shot himself through the Head; he was deeply in Debt for Wooll.'

The wool itself came chiefly from Spanish merino sheep until the Napoleonic War interrupted imports. Cross-breeding of the Cotswold sheep in the 18th century had resulted in a coarser fleece, but the demands of the Stroud clothiers for two to three million fleeces a year in any case far exceeded local production. In the early 19th century merino wool from Germany was preferred and until about 1860 Gloucestershire clothiers travelled to the great wool fairs at Dresden and Breslau. William Playne of Nailsworth even kept a private coach at Calais for his journeys. In 1827 Edward Sheppard of Uley, who also bred merino sheep at Gatcombe Park, was among the first to import Australian merino wool.

The wool was spun by the women and children at home or in the parish workhouses, and afterwards woven at piece rates by handloom weavers. Their workshop was commonly a room downstairs in the house, and the weaver was extremely poor. William Hyde of Horsley in 1753 lived in a four-roomed cottage with a kitchen and workshop downstairs. The kitchen was poorly furnished with an old table, three old chairs and a few cooking utensils. Upstairs in the only bedroom there were a couple of beds, an old chest, trunk and two boxes. The workshop was equipped with a broadloom and tools, the room above it being used for storage. At every trade crisis the weavers were worst hit, and in 1755 William Hyde's neighbours appealed for higher wages on the grounds that 'two Able workmen cannot Earn above Sixpence or Sixpence half penny Each [about $2^1/_2$p] in the space of Fiveteen or Sixteen Houers'.

91 *In 1757 Daniel Packer (d.1769), a wealthy Painswick clothier, insured this fine 18th-century house and the adjoining older wool-store.*

The woven cloth was returned to the clothier's mill where it was fulled, roughened by being passed through a gig mill, and shorn smooth. Dyeing was often put out to a specialist, the Stroud dyers being famed for their scarlets and Uley for blue dyes. An 18th-century mill was, therefore, a simple group of buildings, containing little more than water-powered fulling stocks and gig mills, and warehouses for wool and finished cloth. Nearby there might be workers' cottages and a dye-house. The clothier's own house would be by the mill where he could supervise his men and keep an eye on the drying tenters in the

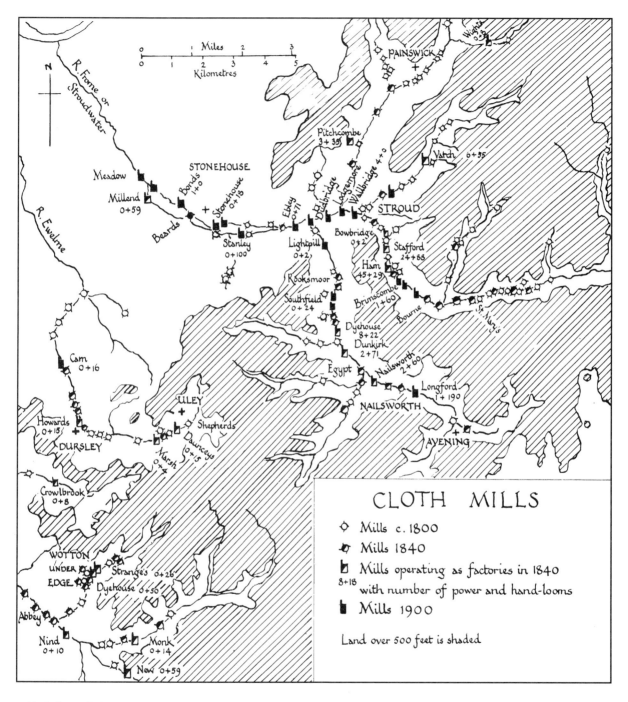

CLOTH MILLS

◇ Mills c. 1800

⚑ Mills 1840

▮ Mills operating as factories in 1840
8+18   with number of power and hand-looms

▮ Mills 1900

Land over 500 feet is shaded

adjoining field (probably called Rack Close) to discourage theft. Although the clothier could arrange his own sales for the English market
all exports were channelled through Blackwell Hall agents in London.
Most Gloucestershire cloths went to the Low Countries, the Levant and

92 *Cloth mills.*

East India Companies in the 18th century, but many were exported to America and Russia in the early 19th century. One of the difficulties facing the clothier was the long delay between buying the wool and selling the cloth, with the uncertainty of not knowing at what price the Blackwell Hall factor would sell.

Gloucestershire clothiers and their workmen were slow to change their methods. Gig mills were chiefly restricted to Gloucestershire from the 16th century and were accepted, but workers fearing unemployment opposed the introduction of shearing machines and spinning machines at the beginning of the 19th century. The biggest change was the introduction of the improved broadloom with flying shuttle about 1795. Weavers feared that because one man could now weave much more cloth unemployment would follow. Even more they resisted working for clothiers who set up looms in the mills, where the weavers would lose their precarious independence. Nevertheless by 1839 there were over a thousand looms in Stroud valley mills. By that time there was a new threat to the weaver's traditional livelihood, for in 1836 Charles Stanton of Stroud bought the first power looms in Gloucestershire. Many new mills were built during the late 18th- and early 19th-century boom. They were

93 *Dunkirk Mills, Nailsworth, 1798-1855, one of the finest cloth mills in Gloucestershire, ceased cloth production about 1890. It was converted into flats in 1992.*

94 *New Mills, Kings-wood, built* c.*1810, was operated as a cloth mill by the Austin family in the early 19th century.*

factories with a complex of buildings including spinning shops, weaving sheds and dye houses. Stanley Mill at Kings Stanley is one of the most striking, being an iron-framed building of 1813 designed to reduce fire hazards.

In 1823 there began a fresh period of crises, accompanied by reduced wages, strikes and riots led by the Woollen Cloth Weavers' Society. In 1825 and 1828 troops were called to the Stroud valley, and again in 1839 when Chartist agitation was expected. The 1823 strike had been settled by Edward Sheppard, chairman of the Clothiers' Committee, agreeing to pay higher wages. A further strike in 1834 cost him £100,000 and in 1837 he went bankrupt. His vast mill at Uley on which he had spent £50,000 on improvements sold for £2,300 and 1,000 people were thrown out of work. Many moved to the iron and coal works of the Forest of Dean and South Wales or emigrated to Australia and America. Despite some recovery in trade mill closures continued, especially after 1875 when broadcloth lost its popularity to the cheaper worsteds. In the early 17th century there had been about 24,000 people employed in the Gloucestershire cloth trade, and about 1800 the Weavers' Society claimed a membership of over twelve thousand. In 1901 only 3,049 were still employed in the industry. In 1839, after the peak of prosperity had passed, 79 mills were working and 58 were closed. In 1901 there were 20 mills, and by 1992 there only survived Cam Mills, Lodgemore Mill at Stroud and Ham Mill at Thrupp.

95 *Stanley Mill, King's Stanley.*

18

Growth of Bristol in the 18th century

During the later 17th century, Bristol had been growing in importance and by 1700 it had become after London both the largest city in England and the largest port. It was from foreign trade that Bristol derived its wealth and influence. As Defoe wrote, 'The merchants of this city not only have the greatest trade, but they trade with a more entire independency upon London than any other town in Britain. And 'tis evident in this particular, (viz.) that whatsoever exportations they make to any part of the world, they are able to bring the full returns back to their own port and dispose of it there'. This prosperity was mainly due to the trade with America and the West Indies, a trade which had been going from strength to strength during the 17th century, and which hinged on a regular supply of slaves from the west coast of Africa.

96 *Bristol Delft ware plate, 1741-2.*

The new trade stimulated the growth of new industries. Defoe travelling through the country in 1725 found Bristol attractive with its new industries of sugar-refining and glass-making. 'There are no less than fifteen glass houses in Bristol which is more than in London,' he wrote. There was a great demand for glass bottles for the water from the Bristol springs, which was shipped all over the world in large quantities. The conical tops of the glass furnaces were a distinctive feature of Bristol's skyline.

The sugar trade with the West Indies kept no less than twenty refineries busy in the city and was partly responsible for one industry—chocolate, which has remained important. In 1729, Walter Churchman took out a patent for making chocolate, a patent which he later sold to Joseph Fry. The famous

family of Wills began the connection with the tobacco industry in 1786, although by this time the manufacture of tobacco had been well established in Bristol. To these industries must be added the manufacture of brass, copper, iron, soap and porcelain.

Bristol was favourably situated at the point where the Bristol Channel, which linked Bristol and the ports of Somerset, Devon, Cornwall and South Wales, joined the River Severn with its network of canals linking Bristol and the West Midlands. From the Midlands, South Wales and the West Country, Bristol continued to draw, as she had done since the Middle Ages, a variety of goods, some of which were the raw materials needed for local industries, whilst other cargoes were sent overseas, in exchange for the products of many lands.

In addition Bristol benefited from a well-organised carrier system which operated from the inns, where fly waggons and vans left daily for London, Birmingham and most of the Midland towns. Messrs. C. & I. Tanner advertised that their London fly waggons set out from the White Lion, St Thomas Street, every day at three o'clock, calling at Bath, Chippenham, Calne, Marlborough, Reading, Maidenhead, Hounslow, Brentford, etc., to the *Rose Inn*, Farringdon Street, and *White Swan*, Holborn Bridge, London. It has been said that this was Bristol's Golden

97 *Broad Quay, Bristol, in the 18th century. Barrels of rum and tierces of tobacco being unloaded and taken away on sledges for no wheeled traffic was allowed in the streets.*

98 *Bristol harbour in the late 18th century by Nicholas Pocock. In the background is the Cathedral, formerly St Augustine's Abbey, before the addition of the nave and western towers in 1877-88.*

Age. Many visitors to the city were attracted by the busy quays. 'You come to a key along the wall, with houses on both sides,' wrote Pope to Martha Blount in 1733, 'and in the middle of the street as far as you can see, hundreds of ships, their masts as thick as they can stand by one another, which is the oddest and most surprising sight imaginable.' A view of the harbour shows the quay lined with a row of gabled houses, the river crowded with sails and masts of sailing craft, casks of rum and molasses and wooden drums of tobacco being unloaded on to the sledge-like carriers drawn by horses.

At the beginning of the 18th century Bristol looked very much as it had done during the Middle Ages. The city was still walled and entrance could be gained only through the various gates. As late as 1734, Temple Gate was rebuilt. The streets of the city were much as they had been when the traffic was exclusively carried by means of pack horses and when the wealthiest travellers moved about on horseback. The average breadth of the busiest thoroughfares was under 20 feet. The main streets were paved with rough blocks of stone and the cost of repairing them fell on each householder, who was required to pay the pitcher to mend his portion of the road. When Celia Fiennes visited Bristol in 1685 she found 'the buildings of the town so high, most of timber, the streets narrow and somewhat darkish, because the roomes on the upper storeys are more jutting out soe contracts the streete and light'.

The rich merchants were still content to live on their business premises, their cellars acting as warehouses for their goods. Because the streets were honeycombed with cellars, no wheeled traffic was allowed in the town and horse-drawn sledges were used instead, which Pepys noted as a curious novelty in a city that in most respects reminded him of London. Life in the city was far from comfortable, sanitation received scanty attention, the water supplies were inadequate, and the streets were rarely cleaned. The housing problem by this time must have been acute for the

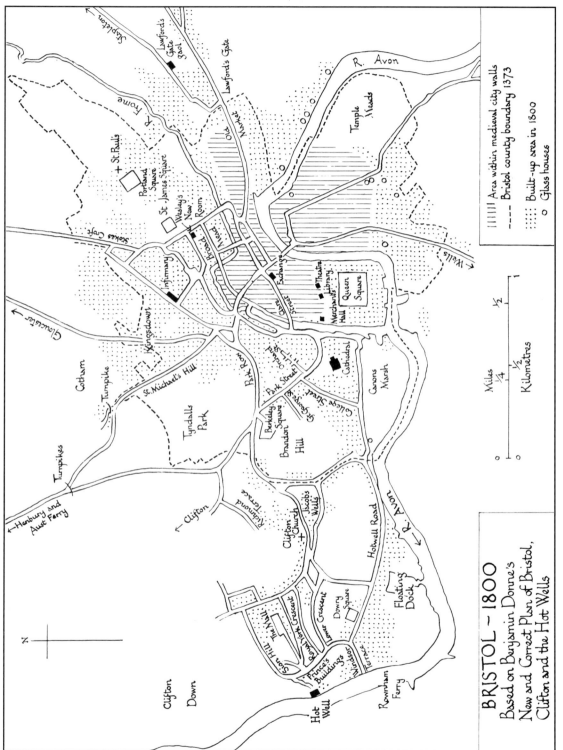

BRISTOL ~ 1800
Based on Benjamin Donne's
New and Correct Plan of Bristol,
Clifton and the Hot Wells

||||| Area within medieval city walls
--- Bristol county boundary 1373
:::: Built-up area in 1800
o Glass houses

Miles
¼   ½   1
Kilometres
½

99 *Bristol Docks in 1800.*

100 *Theatre Royal,*
Bristol.

population had risen to 20,000, yet it was still concentrated in and around the old city walls. The dissolution of the monasteries in the 16th century meant that much of the land encircling the city was released from the control of the religious houses and available for development. Progress, however, was slow. The site of the castle had been built over, the gardens of the medieval town had been filled in, and still the city became more and more cramped and overcrowded. In fact by the end of the century the population had more than trebled.

During the 18th century the character of the whole city was changed by extensive building. Part of the city's wealth was spent in improvement schemes and for the first time 'planning' made its appearance. Fine Georgian town houses were laid out in squares, such as Queen Square, St James's Square and Portland Square. The Georgian House in Great George Street with its fine rooms and ample kitchens is typical of its period, being furnished with furniture, glass and porcelain such as might have been there when it was the home of Charles Pinney, a West Indian merchant.

The centre of the city was largely rebuilt: new streets, such as Orchard Street, Clare Street and Bridge Street were made and many others widened. As Donne's map of 1773 illustrates the physical changes in the first half of the century, so Ashmead's map of about 1813 shows the enormous development which had taken place in the second. In 1704 the Corporation re-built the Council House, and the merchants, who wanted

101 *The   Georgian*
House, Bristol, originally
the home of the merchant,
Charles Pinney.   The
eating room.

a more dignified meeting place, commissioned John Wood, the elder, of Bath to build the Exchange in 1742. About the same time a new library was erected, replacing the original foundation of 1613. In 1766 the Theatre Royal was opened, and is now the oldest theatre in the country with a continuous existence.

At the Tolzey, under the shadow of All Saints and Christchurch, merchants and traders gathered together, making bargains which they clinched 'on the nail', that is, on the brass pillars which were used as tables and now stand on the pavement in front of the Exchange. Nearby in coffee houses men met to exchange news and get a glimpse of a newspaper. One of the first newspapers to be published outside London was the *Bristol Post Boy* started by William Bonny in 1702. From the *Bush Inn* in Corn Street, famed for its entertainment and hospitality, and the *White Lion* in Broad Street, where Sir Thomas Lawrence's father was

102 *Bristol Exchange and All Saints church. Engraving c.1825. On the pavement are four bronze baluster tables which were used by the merchants for making money payments and are said to have originated the expression 'paying on the nail'.*

landlord the mail coaches left daily for London, Birmingham, Exeter and many other places. It was at the *Bush* that Mr. Winkle in Dickens's *Pickwick Papers* stayed on his visit to the city seeking the lost Arabella Allen.

There were in addition those visitors who came to Bristol to take the waters at the Hotwell, which was about one mile from the city by the side of the River Avon. The hot springs which flowed out of the cliff face near the entrance to the Avon Gorge rose rapidly to fame after a visit by Charles II's queen, Catherine of Braganza. By the early years of the 18th century the Hotwell was a fashionable resort, with its colonnade, assembly rooms and Vauxhall Gardens. During the season, the average company at public breakfasts and at evening balls numbered two hundred persons or more. Addison, Cowper, Pope and Sheridan were among the famous literary figures who visited the spa. There in 1728, the *Beggars' Opera* was played, when Gay himself was present.

19

Wesley and Whitefield

103 *John Wesley's statue, Bristol.*

104 *John Wesley's chapel, Bristol, where Wesley lived. The communion table is the one used by him and he presented the clock.*

The spread of religious dissent had been accelerated by the upheavals of the Civil War and Interregnum. After the restoration of Charles II the Act of Uniformity 1662 drew a sharp distinction between the Anglican Church and those who were not willing to conform to its articles. Many parsons were ejected from their livings, some taking their followers with them and founding new Independent or Congregational meetings like those at Nailsworth and Mitcheldean.

An older established group of dissenters were the Baptists, one of whose chapels, complete with 17th-century fittings, survives at Tewkesbury, a town where three-quarters of the population were non-conformists in 1676. Despite their unpopularity the followers of George Fox, nicknamed Quakers in 1650, also flourished, especially in villages remote from Anglican churches like Frenchay and Nailsworth. The rigid rules and mutual help required by the Society of Friends, coupled with their industry and modest ways, helped to make successful businessmen of many Quakers.

In Bristol, Puritanism found a ready home, and flourished despite persecution. It was said that there were more dissenters in Bristol than in the whole of the West of England, and that their meetings were attended by thousands of people. In 1640 the first open and independent congregation was founded, mainly through the efforts of Dorothy Hazzard, who was the wife of the vicar of St Ewen's. Their house became a recognised meeting place, and a place of lodging for Puritans on their way to New England. Out of this group came Broadmead Baptist church, which survives today. At the same time, many prominent citizens were members of the Presbyterian church which established itself in a chapel in Lewin's Mead. This independent congregation in 1775 became Unitarian.

The first Quakers to come to Bristol were John Audland and Thomas Airey in 1654. They preached first of all to the Independents and Baptists who were already meeting outside the parish churches. Later the Quakers had a Meeting House in Broadmead, and George Fox made it the base of his work in the West. In 1670 the Quakers bought the house of the Dominican Friars, and this, under the name of Quakers Friars, remained the chief meeting house of the Society of Friends for nearly three hundred years. Among the leading Quakers was William Penn, founder of Pennsylvania, whose chief motive in founding Pennsylvania was a desire to rescue some of his brethren from persecution and provide a haven where Quakerism might flourish.

105 *George Whitefield (1714-70), the leader of the Calvinistic Methodists, was born at Gloucester.*

In the 18th century it was undoubtedly John Wesley who created the greatest stir in the religious life of Bristol. John and Charles Wesley and George Whitefield had been friends at Oxford, where they had been members of a society of young men known as 'Methodists', who were anxious for a spiritual revival in a country where religion seemed dead. In 1737 George Whitefield came to Bristol to preach, whilst the Wesley brothers went to America. Two years later John Wesley arrived in Bristol to carry on this work of preaching in the open air. At his first meeting 3,000 people gathered round to listen.

Their fire, zeal and eloquence aroused jealousy and hostility in the Established Church and Wesley was barred from most parish churches. Once he preached in Clifton church and on one or two occasions in Temple church. His continued exclusion from most of the city churches and the growth of his following made it imperative for proper premises to be found for preaching and worship. Within a year of his arrival in Bristol, John Wesley took land in the Horsefair and had built there the New Room—the first Methodist church. The first service was held in 1739. His ties with Bristol were strengthened in 1749 when his brother Charles, the great hymn writer, settled in the city.

In his famous *Journal* he speaks of the long journeys he made, of the inns where he preached, of the savage miners at Kingswood, where he started his boys' school, and of the French prisoners that he visited at Knowle, Bristol, where they were confined in filth and without proper clothing and bedding, so 'that they died like rotten sheep'. To remedy this he collected more warm clothing and started a public subscription. During the forty years of his ministry he travelled thousands of miles on

106 *Kingswood School.*

107 *Randwick Methodist chapel, 1807, rebuilt 1824. The Stroud clothworking villages were a centre of the nonconformity and both Whitefield and Wesley had preached in the village.*

horseback preaching the gospel wherever he went. At times the task must have been depressing, as on the occasion in 1756 when he visited Coleford. 'Examining the little society, I found them grievously harassed by disputations. Anabaptists were on one side and Quakers on the other', and the establishment of permanent congregations with churches and regular meeting places mostly took place after his death in 1791.

George Whitefield probably enjoyed greater success as a preacher in his own lifetime. Born and educated in Gloucester he became, like the Wesley brothers, an ordained clergyman in the Church of England, and for his first short appointment was at Stonehouse in 1737. Also like the Wesleys he travelled widely in America as well as England, but it was at Kingswood and Hanham that he first preached in 1739 in the open to groups of miners. His energy was prodigious, preaching in churches when invited or in fields when obstructed. In 1739, for instance, he rode from London to Cirencester and Gloucester.

> June 28th,—Preached morning and evening in the field at Gloucester.
>
> 29th,—in my brother's field [at Gloucester] to a large and affected congregation; then to above 3,000 in the street at Painswick.
>
> 30th,—On the Bowling-green at Stroud, in the morning to 2,000; in the evening to a large congregation at Gloucester.
>
> July 1st,—At seven in my brother's field, again at 11, and then to Randwick, the church was quite full, and about 2,000 were in the churchyard, who by taking down the window behind the pulpit, were able to hear. Many wept sorely. Hastened to [Minchin] Hampton Common, and found no less than 20,000 on horseback and foot, ready to hear me'.

The first meeting house built by his followers was at Kingswood in 1739, and in his lifetime other tabernacles were built at Bristol in 1753 and Rodborough in 1766. After his death in America in 1770 his patron Selina, Countess of Huntingdon, continued to build and endow chapels.

None of this missionary activity, which spread rapidly in the early 19th century, infecting at last the Church of England also, was achieved without opposition and persecution. Quakers suffered repeated insults, fines and imprisonment; Charles Wesley was stoned at St Briavels and Whitefield was assaulted at Minchinhampton. At Newnham about 1800, services were interrupted and a chapel broken into, 'the forms and pulpit stolen, broken and thrown into the Severn, and the windows of the house demolished'. The persecuted congregations thrived and today empty chapels in remote hamlets or the poorer quarters of the towns bear witness of the high tide of nonconformist zeal in Victorian times.

20

County Town

The city of Gloucester, though always overshadowed by Bristol, was the main centre of inland trade in the region, strategically placed at a hub of communications at the lowest bridging point over the Severn. The concentration of its varied industries and commerce was unmatched in either the cloth-manufacturing valleys or other market towns and it held an unrivalled position in the shire as the county town.

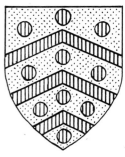

108 *Gloucester city arms.*

The city suffered severely for its support of Parliament in the Civil War. The corporation had fired 241 houses in the suburbs at the outset of the siege, Royalist guns had damaged the city centre and five city churches were pulled down, one during the siege and four subsequently. Its trade had been disrupted and the wealthy Royalist merchants and county gentry deserted it. Faced with increased numbers of the poor, who formed one-quarter of the population about 1700, the corporation had impoverished itself by defence costs during the war. Some labour-intensive industries picked up, such as pinmaking and brickmaking, and the corporation had built a new tolsey and market halls between 1648 and 1660, but the long-term effects were felt for many years. The community remained divided by faction for long after the war, the population was static at about 5,000 for a century and not until the end of the 18th century were the suburbs rebuilt.

The restoration of the monarchy in 1660 was celebrated by the corporation with fireworks and wine running from the three public conduits, but such a show of loyalty did not save it from the revenge of the Crown and country gentry. In 1662-3 the town walls were demolished, 35 aldermen, councillors and the fiercely puritan town clerk, John Dorney, were removed and the in-shire of neighbouring countryside granted in 1483 was transferred to the county. New royal charters extended the grip of the Crown and gentry over the corporation of 1664.

With a continuing powerful minority of dissenters and memories of the Civil War still fresh it was hardly surprising that Gloucester should mirror national controversy over the politics and religion of later Stuart kings. In 1671-2 alderman Robert Fielding led strong opposition to the election of a royalist mayor, Henry Fowler, with the result that a new charter in 1672 further tightened loyalist control of the city. Later feuding between Whigs and Tories ran high after the 1688 revolution. At the cathedral in 1679 a new prebendary, Edward Fowler, took exception to

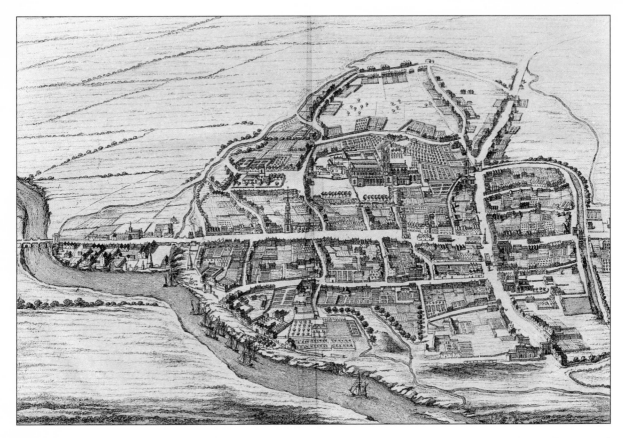

109 *Gloucester city, 1712. Kip's view shows the line of the city ditch and walls, with the town gates, market and other buildings in the middle of the main streets, the churches and former friaries, fine houses and gardens, Castle gaol and nearby quays with the glassworks, sugar refinery and Severn trows.*

a stained glass window depicting the Holy Trinity and, when obstructed by the cathedral's High Church treasurer, Abraham Gregory, in having it destroyed, exclaimed, 'I will go and do it presently my selfe' and with a long pole dashed it to pieces. Abraham Gregory was further outraged in 1689 when the eccentric Whiggish cathedral organist, Stephen Jefferies, closed the public thanksgiving service for William of Orange's deliverance of the kingdom from popery with a triumphant rendering of the lively anti-Jacobite air 'Lilliburlero'.

Nevertheless, as passions subsided into political rivalry the combination of reforming nonconformist energy and gentry interests strengthened Gloucester's rôle as the county town. By 1700 it had regained its long-established position as a regional market for grain and malt, to which cheese and cider were later to be added, and as a distributive centre by river and road for luxury goods and manufactures imported from London and Bristol, coal from the West Midlands, salt from Droitwich and timber from the Baltic. Its own industries grew apace, especially pinmaking, which employed 1,500 mostly poor workers at the end of the century, brickmaking and the Rudhall family's bell foundry in Oxbode Lane which, it was claimed, made 4,000 bells between 1684 and 1789. For much of the same period the conical towers of a glassworks and

sugar refinery dominated the quay-
side before they closed in face of
competition from Bristol.

More enduring were the service trades and professions, the bank-
ers such as James Wood, whose
bank, opened about 1716, was the
last private bank in Gloucester to
close in 1836 on the death of his
grandson Jemmy, notorious as a
wealthy miser, the lawyers attracted
by assize, quarter sessions and
ecclesiastical courts, booksellers and
printers, including Robert Raikes
the elder, who began the *Gloucester Journal* in 1722, physicians,
schoolmasters and innholders.

110 *Westgate Street,
Gloucester, 1825.*

Their influence brought material changes to the city. During the
course of the 18th century the corporation, despite its reputation for self-
indulgence, improved water supplies, widened the main streets, developed the quay and rebuilt the tolsey, market halls, poorhouses and gaol.
Fashionable houses with fine gardens were built or refronted in brick,
especially from the beginning of the century near the cathedral and
castle, where bordering some of the worst slums the county gentry resided
for part of the year, drawn by the social events of the assizes, autumn
race meetings from the 1720s, triennial music festivals from 1718 and
intermittent balls, lectures and plays. Not until the end of the century
with the emergence of Cheltenham and the London season did Gloucester lose its attraction as a social centre, but by then the city was already
turning its attention to industrial expansion.

Investment in communications by canals, turnpike roads, tramroads
and railways was the key to Gloucester's 19th-century growth. It was led
by men such as John Philpotts (d. 1849), barrister, Liberal M.P. and
developer, William Price (d. 1838), timber merchant and builder, and his
son W.P. Price (d. 1891), another Liberal M.P. Foreign imports made
Gloucester in 1851 the third largest grain port in the country after London
and Glasgow. The timber trade continued to flourish, encouraging the
subsidiary industries of shipbuilding, carriage-building and matchmaking,
and employing 1,000 workers by 1871. Pinmaking and bellfounding were
replaced by new foundries in the 1850s and 1860s, employing a further
1,000 workmen, and by the Gloucester Railway Carriage and Wagon
company, formed in 1860 and the city's dominant single employer. In the
century from 1801 to 1901 Gloucester's population expanded over sixfold
from 7,579 to 47,955, its central streets were lined with new public
buildings, shops, banks and offices, and its new-built suburbs sprawled
eastwards.

21

Georgian Cheltenham

Cheltenham, which became the leading spa in the county, had a humble
origin. In 1718 a saline spring, on the site of Cheltenham Ladies' College
and well known to the inhabitants of the small market town, attracted
the attention of its owner, William Mason. According to local legend his
notice was first drawn to the spring by pigeons which regularly fed there,
and today the town's coat of arms incorporates pigeons within its design.

111 *Georgian Cheltenham.*

The legend is possibly well founded for when the first pump room was built in 1738 by Henry Skillicorne it was ornamented with pigeons. Skillicorne, a retired Manx sea-captain, married Mason's daughter, and he can be credited with the foundation of modern Cheltenham. Apart from building the first Pump Room, where annually for 10 years he entertained over 600 visitors, he laid out the tree-lined Well Walk approaching the well, which set the example for the town's later avenues, contributing so much to its graceful appearance. In 1776 his son William built at the well a good sized Assembly Room for parties and balls, and in 1781 Bayshill House for Lord Fauconberg—Cheltenham's first large villa. The early small ballrooms and theatre were replaced by an Assembly Room in the High Street designed by Henry Holland in 1781-4, and a theatre in the same street for J.B. Watson. In 1781 Simon Moreau came from Bath as Master of Ceremonies to direct the programme of social events during the summer season. The promoters of the spa were faced with many setbacks. Travel to the town was hindered by bad roads and accommodation in the primitive market town was inadequate. Fewer visitors arrived than were hoped for, and attempts to improve amenities often aroused factional opposition. Worst of all, there was a shortage of spa water.

Then in 1788 George III and his family visited Cheltenham for five weeks, staying at Fauconberg's house. According to Mary Yorke of Forthampton there was a great desire in Cheltenham to secure the royal visit in order to revive interest in the spa. The king enjoyed simple pleasures and, although Cheltenham could not cure his disease, the royal holiday was a great success. 'Their life at Cheltenham is perfectly quiet, the King rises and drinks the Water at six every morning and at nine appears upon the Public Walks with the Princesses, but they none of

113 *Caryatid, Cheltenham.*

114 *George III at the Royal Well.*

them appear again at any Public Meeting except Church; where one wag had been amused that the singers chose an anthem on the 1st verse of the 72nd psalm.' ('Give the King judgement, O God, and righteousness to the King's son'—the rakish future Prince Regent).

Apart from numberless excursions on foot and horse in and about the town, when the king willingly chatted to anybody he met, longer trips were made. The royal party, ably organised by Sir George Onesiphorus Paul, inspected a cloth mill at Woodchester, but a proposed voyage by barge on the Stroudwater canal was cancelled because 'the Queen would be alarmed with the water'. At Tewkesbury the king scrambled up the Mythe Hill to admire the view, and he attended the Three Choirs Festival (held that year at Worcester) to listen to his favourite music by Handel. Finally, as Fanny Burney in attendance on the queen recorded, the party left. 'All Cheltenham was drawn out into the High Street, the gentles on one side and the commons on the other, and a band playing God save the King ... . And there ends the Cheltenham adventure.'

For Cheltenham the adventure was just beginning. The spa became immediately fashionable and many famous people came to take the waters, of whom the popular Duke of Wellington was the most notable. Among those who ministered to the seasonal influx of cure-seeking visitors was Edward Jenner, the Berkeley doctor who discovered vaccination against smallpox in 1796. The water shortage was overcome by sinking additional wells, the earliest being called the King's Well, at the instance of George III himself. In 1791 the lower end of the Promenade was built, extending into a splendid tree-lined walk to a new Sherborne Spa in 1818. New lodging houses were built in Cambray, and after the end of the Napoleonic War the Montpellier and Lansdown estates were built in

115 *Lansdown Crescent, Cheltenham. Henry Thompson and his son Pearson developed their Montpellier and Lansdown property between 1809 and 1835. Most of the estate was designed between 1825 and 1830 by J.B. Papworth, a London architect, as 'the first English garden city'; Lansdown Crescent was completed by R.W. and C. Jearrad.*

116 *Suffolk Square, Cheltenham by J.B. Papworth, 1825.*

the fashionable Regency style. On the north side of the High Street Joseph Pitt, M.P. (1759-1843), a successful Cirencester lawyer and speculator, started Pittville in 1823 on land inclosed from the open fields in 1806. There John Forbes designed the town's most spectacular Pump Room in Pittville Park, opened in 1830, but its development was slow because of a general financial crisis. At the lower end of the High Street the rows of artisans' and servants' cottages were crowded and unsavoury. In a huge building boom the population rose from 3,076 in 1801 to 22,942 in 1831.

Under the patronage of Colonel W.F. Berkeley, later Earl Fitzhardinge, the theatre, racing and hunting flourished, together with balls, musical promenades and card playing, to make Cheltenham 'the merriest sick resort on earth'. Not everyone approved. William Cobbett condemned the town as 'this resort of the lame and lazy, the gourmandising and guzzling, the bilious and the nervous', while from his pulpit in the parish church Francis Close (1797-1882) preached eloquently against racing and the theatre, Tractarians and Roman Catholics, Sunday trains and Socialists. By the time he left to become Dean of Carlisle in 1856 Close and his Evangelical supporters had converted Cheltenham into a rather staid and snobbish residential town.

Elsewhere in the county spas were established in emulation of Cheltenham's success. All were failures. Gloucester Spa on the south of the city was discovered in 1814 and was still advertised in the 1840s, and some attractive houses remain in its neighbourhood. Spas at Newent, Ashchurch, Stonehouse and Stow had shorter lives and, apart from the spa house outside Stow on the road to Lower Swell, are now hard to trace.

117 *Cheltenham ironwork.*

22

Roads and Travellers

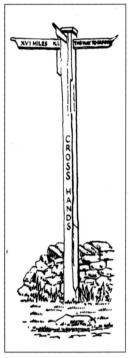

Since Roman times three main routes have crossed Gloucestershire—from London to Gloucester and South Wales, from London to Bristol and Ireland, and between Bristol, Gloucester and the Midlands. The actual course of the routes has varied. The medieval way north from Bristol, for instance, passed through Iron Acton and Cam, or even through the upland towns of Chipping Sodbury and Wotton-under-Edge, rather than through the Vale. From London the road by Oxford and Northleach to Gloucester was used until Abingdon bridge was built in the early 15th century, after which most travellers preferred to ride up the Thames Valley to Cirencester.

In 1289 Richard de Swinfield, Bishop of Hereford, took neither main route on his journey to London. From Hereford he went by Ledbury, Newent and Gloucester at the rate of seven to twelve miles a day until he reached his estate at Prestbury, where he stayed for Christmas. His party consisted of thirty to forty horses and baggage carts, and was accompanied by a pack of hounds for hunting at Prestbury. Servants rode ahead to prepare for the bishop's arrival, and were dispatched to buy fish in Gloucester and ale from wayside taverns or farms. Better progress was made across the Cotswolds by Coln St Aldwyn to Faringdon, and thence to Wantage and Reading. On the return journey in late January 1290 they reached Prestbury from Lechlade in one day (a distance of 22 miles), but only at the cost of leaving behind a waggon that had broken down.

118 *Signpost near Chipping Campden.*

The bishop's travels must have taken him up and down the steep Cotswold edge, but hills like Birdlip or Toghill were no great hindrance to horse and foot traffic. It was the growing numbers of wheeled vehicles in the 17th and 18th centuries which found such roads too steep and narrow. In 1698 Celia Fiennes, riding on horseback, 'came to Nymphsffield after haveing ascended a very steep narrow and stony hill 10 mile to Nympsfield, all bad way', and nearly a century later Arthur Young, the agricultural reformer journeying to South Wales from Gloucester, commented that 'in many places the road is so very narrow, that my chaise with great difficulty got through it without rising on the banks'. In the Vale the main road between Gloucester and Bristol was so deep in mud in 1776 that the Gloucestershire historian, Samuel Rudder, was told that a horse had been nearly smothered. Conditions were little better in the Cotswolds. The stone was too soft to withstand the weight of the traffic and the local practice of excavating stone for repairs from the roadside converted the roads into causeways with dangerous pits on each side.

In such circumstances it is not surprising that stage coaches in the early 18th century took three days from Bristol to London. Of all the difficulties, the Aust ferry between Bristol and Wales was the most hazardous, and Daniel Defoe abandoned his proposed tour of the Welsh Marches when he saw it. 'The sea was so Broad,' he wrote, 'the Fame of the Bore of the Tide so formidable, the Wind also made the Water so rough, and which was worse, the Boats to carry over both Man and Horse appear'd so very mean, that in short none of us car'd to venture.'

The establishment of the turnpike trusts, charging tolls for the repair of the roads, resulted in little immediate improvement. The earliest trust in Gloucestershire was set up in 1698 for the steep roads leading from Gloucester towards London. The road from Bristol to London, commonly called the Bath Road, was turnpiked soon afterwards in 1727, and in the first half of the 18th century Turnpike Acts were passed for the maintenance of the main routes between Bristol and Gloucester, and from each of those cities to the capital.

There was violent opposition to the payment of tolls, particularly from the hauliers. Miners from Kingswood Forest destroyed all the gates between Gloucester and Bristol in 1734, and when in 1731 Dean Forest miners wrecked a gate near Mitcheldean they 'Swore if any more was erected they would Come again and Cutt that down also ... . By Which meanes The Keeperes are Soe Terrified, that they will not ask, nor Demand any Toll'. As the system spread from the middle of the century many more gates were built to prevent evasion, and toll-keepers' houses remain, for example, at Dyrham, Huntley, Tewkesbury and many other places. Dozens of milestones erected by the trusts also survive, placed along the roads in a successful attempt to measure and standardise distances—for, as Celia Fiennes remarked of Gloucestershire miles in 1698, 'they are pretty long miles ... its 8 mile beyond [Herefordshire] to Glocester town (tho' in most places near London this would be reckon'd 20 miles)'.

Completely new main roads were constructed in a few notable areas, such as the industrial valleys near Stroud or the Forest of Dean. In the Forest the Crown spent over £11,000 between 1761 and 1786 in making two main roads which were turnpiked shortly afterwards. One of these running from Mitcheldean to Monmouth was praised by the Honourable John Byng in 1781 as 'the most beautiful I ever took', and it is still one

120 *Milestone, Cain-cross.*

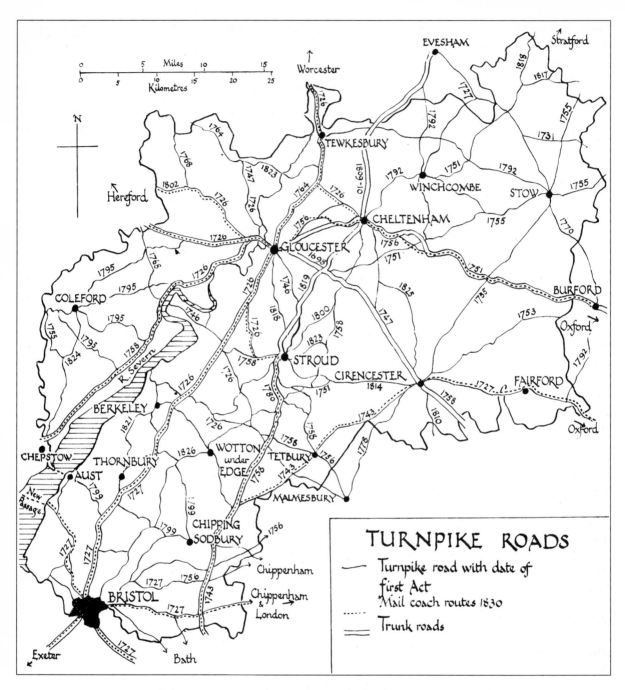

121 *Turnpike roads.*

of the most attractive main roads in the county, especially in the autumn. The importance of the growing spa town of Cheltenham is indicated in the new main roads built from the town to Winchcombe (1792), Evesham (1809-10), Bath (1819-20) and Cirencester (1825), as well as the major improvements to the London (1824) and Gloucester (1809 and 1825) roads. Although the last had been a turnpike since 1756 its condition was appalling, and in 1789, the year after George III stayed in Cheltenham, it was 'scarcely fit for the meanest of their Majesties' subjects to travel on—AND PAY FOR: and is much less suitable for their Majesties themselves and their amiable family to trust their own persons upon'.

Since on one occasion the mail coach had taken two hours to cover this 10-mile stretch of road the improvements achieved by the mail services were remarkable. In 1741 Ralph Allen of Bath, the Post Office Comptroller, had initiated a daily service between London and Bristol. The bags were usually carried by young and ill-mounted post-boys who took two days over the journey. Unarmed and sometimes dishonest they were no match for such rogues as Richard Carey, who, armed with two loaded pistols and a sword, was arrested near Berkeley in 1748 on suspicion of being a highwayman. A succeeding Comptroller, John Palmer, who also came from Bath, radically reformed this dilatory and unreliable service by introducing the fast and light mail coach. With four inside passengers only, and carrying a guard armed with a blunderbuss to deter raiders and a horn to warn the toll-gate keepers to open the gates, the first mail coach in the country left Bristol at 4 p.m. on 2 August 1784. It drew up in London on schedule only 16 hours later, vindicating Palmer against his critics who had declared it impossible. On the improved roads of the 19th century even faster speeds were regularly achieved, and the Bristol Mail's timetable allowed it only 12 hours including stops for the 114-mile journey.

The road improvements were obtained by specialist engineers. Thomas Telford surveyed the road from London by Gloucester to South Wales in 1824, and his recommendations included a new line between Gloucester and Cheltenham not built until 1968-9. He designed two important bridges over the Severn, the Mythe Bridge at Tewkesbury (1823-6), 'the handsomest bridge built under my direction', and Over Bridge at Gloucester (1826-9). J.L. McAdam was personally responsible for some local roads, for he was surveyor of the Bristol Turnpike Trust from 1815 to 1824. Together with his son he reformed the administration of the Trust and supervised some two hundred road improvements in the Bristol area. His method of constructing a resilient and well-drained road surface was much cheaper than Telford's solid stone foundations, and is still in favour with highway engineers.

THE OXFORD AND CHELTENHAM COACH, "BLENHEIM,"

Leaves the MITRE HOTEL, OXFORD, every Monday, Wednesday and Friday, at 2·30; returning from the PLOUGH HOTEL, CHELTENHAM, every Tuesday, Thursday and Saturday at 2·30.

Fares Inside or Out.	Miles.	UP.	o'clock.	Fares Inside or Out.	Miles.	DOWN.	o'clock
		OXFORD	2·30			CHELTENHAM ..	2·30
1/.	5	*EYNSHAM......	·3·0	1/.	5	*ANDOVERSFORD	3·10
	11	WITNEY	3·45	2/3	12	*NORTHLEACH ..	3·55
2/3	14¼	*MINSTER LOVELL	4·15	3/9	18	*BARRINGTON ..	4·35
3/9	22¼	*BARRINGTON ..	5·0	5/3	26	*MINSTER LOVELL	5·25
5/3	28¼	*NORTHLEACH ..	5·40		29¼	WITNEY	5·45
6/6	35¼	*ANDOVERSFORD	6·20	6/6	35¼	*EYNSHAM......	6·25
7/6	40¼	CHELTENHAM ..	7·0	7/6	40¼	OXFORD	7·0

Box Seat 2/6 extra each way.

INTERMEDIATE FARES are charged at an average rate of 3d. per mile, but not less than 1/. taken. 28lbs. of Luggage allowed. 1d. per lb. afterwards.

Parcels carried at low rates and delivered with the greatest punctuality.

* CHANGE HORSES.

122 *Cheltenham-Oxford coach timetable, 1879. The old coaching route had not been replaced by a railway line. The single fare was 7s. 6d.*

23

Canals and Railways

Despite turnpike road improvements it was still difficult and costly to convey heavy goods by land. Spanish wool from Bristol, for example, cost $1^1/_2$p a hundredweight to carry by river to Gloucester, and 3p a hundredweight from Gloucester to Stroud by road in the summer, and half as much again in winter. The importance of the river trade between the Midlands, Gloucester and Bristol was emphasised in the winter of 1607-8 when the river froze at Tewkesbury and no coal or wood reached the town, and trade with Bristol was stopped.

The earliest proposals to extend the range of waterborne transport were made late in the 17th century. The River Avon between Bath and Bristol was made navigable in 1724-7, and an Act of Parliament was passed to improve the River Frome or Stroudwater in 1730. Opposition to the first scheme came from the colliers and hauliers who feared the loss of their trade, and to the Stroudwater from clothiers who anticipated loss of water for driving their mills. The influential clothiers were successful in their opposition, and a scheme devised in 1759 by Thomas Bridges, 'a chimerical crack-brained fellow', to run a shuttle service of container ships, which would transfer their cargoes at each level, was an expensive failure. It was not until 1779 that a canal was substituted for

123 *Brimscombe, near Stroud, 1828. A busy scene at the interchange port between the Stroudwater Canal and the Thames and Severn Canal.*

the original proposal to deepen the river, and Severn river trows were able to work up to Stroud.

While the Stroudwater canal was still under construction interest revived in a link between the Severn and Thames. Robert Whitworth surveyed a route in 1782. His estimate of the cost was £128,000, but the proposal came at the height of the mania for investment in canals and the money was raised rapidly. The construction of the 29-miles long canal was carried out at an equally impressive speed. The chief

124 *Berkeley Canal at Frampton-on-Severn.*

engineering problem was the Sapperton tunnel, which Whitworth had refused to estimate precisely, as it was 'an uncertain piece of Business in point of Expense'. Gangs of miners worked day and night every day of the week to blast and dig their way through the hillside.

In November 1789 the first boat passed through into the Thames from the Severn. Nearly all the laden boats travelled in that direction, most of them carrying coal. In 1834, 34,578 tons were carried eastwards, compared with only 3,616 tons from London. The canal was not an outstanding success. Water levels often became so low because of leaks that the canal had to be closed in summer, and in addition boats had to cope with the bad navigation of both the Severn and the upper Thames. The Kennet and Avon canal, opened in 1810 from Bath to Reading, was a more direct link between London and the Severn and had the added advantage of serving Bristol as well. In 1792 Bristol had been the scene of no less than three canal ventures—from Bristol to Gloucester, Bristol to Taunton and a canal linking Bristol with Southampton and London. That none came to anything was at least partly the result of the war with France and the accompanying financial depression.

The geographic and economic basis for the Bristol to Gloucester canal was not altogether unsound and had the circumstances been more favourable it might well have been built, for worse schemes were carried out at about the same time. As it happened the hazardous navigation of the Severn with its tides, shifting sandbanks and shallow stone reefs was not overcome until the construction of the shorter Gloucester and Berkeley canal. The Act was obtained in 1793, but the estimates of £121,329 for its construction were wildly optimistic, and were almost completely spent in digging the Gloucester docks and first few miles to Hardwicke in 1799. The original terminus of the canal at Berkeley was shortened in favour of Sharpness and the canal was opened at last in 1827. It soon proved successful. By the middle of the century the annual tonnage carried was about 500,000 and it continued to increase, to treble that amount in the 1940s.

125 *Horse tramway wagon.*

All the canals were affected by railway competition. As early as 1811 the short Coombe Hill canal was deprived of the carriage of coal and building materials for Cheltenham by the construction of a horse tramway from Gloucester docks. The directors of the Herefordshire and Gloucester canal were considering a sale to the West Midland Railway even before their canal had reached Hereford in 1845. The Thames and Severn company challenged the Great Western Railway by cutting tolls and by attempting to form a rival railway company as they watched their revenue drop from £11,000 in 1841 to £2,874 in 1855. The Great Western bought the canal in 1882, and after a short revival early in this century the canal was finally closed in 1933.

Railways had developed from primitive tracks like that of Charles Jones at the Sapperton tunnel in 1784, where a visitor described 'a stage or platform laid for the wheels of waggons to run on, and from a shoulder which is given to the wheel, the wagon ... is prevented from slipping off'. These tramroads were developed in mining districts early in the 19th century, and in Gloucestershire two lines were laid in the Forest of Dean in 1809-10, one of which from Bullo Pill had the first railway tunnel in the world. In the Bristol coalfield two lines from Coalpit Heath were opened in 1828, one of which four years later became the first steam railway in the county.

On several occasions prior to 1832 citizens of Bristol had considered proposals for the construction of a railroad to connect Bristol with London, but nothing tangible resulted until Richard Guppy, George Jones, John Harford and William Tothill, local influential business men, took steps to bring the scheme to fruition. After the opening of a line from London to Bristol in 1840, Bristol rapidly developed as an important railway centre of communication. Isambard K. Brunel was the engineer, and the works which he constructed for the Great Western Railway in the neighbourhood of Bristol were amongst the most intricate. Within the first mile eastward, bridges had to be built to carry the line over the

126 *Temple Meads station, Bristol: the train shed designed by I.K. Brunel. The railway link with London was completed in 1841.*

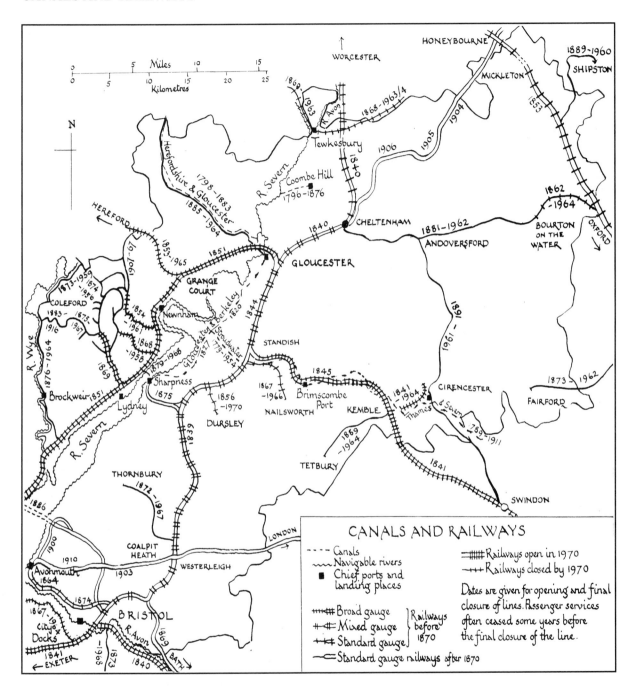

127 *Canals and Railways.*

Floating Harbour, Feeder Canal and the New Cut. The first trains took four hours to reach London from Bristol compared with twelve to sixteen hours by mail coach.

The first goods depot erected by the Great Western Railway at Temple Meads in 1840 catered for 209 waggons. Before the coming of the railway, carriers transported goods to all parts. In the Bristol directory of 1820 are listed the names of 176 carriers, many of whom left Bristol daily for London, Birmingham and most of the towns in the Midlands and West Country. It was this aspect of Bristol's trade that interested Daniel Defoe who wrote: 'the shopkeepers, who in general, are all wholesale men have so great an inland trade among the western counties, that they maintain carriers just as the London tradesmen do.'

Between 1840 and 1860 there was constructed a network of lines radiating from Bristol and Gloucester. In 1865, Temple Meads became the centre for the three railway companies then serving Bristol, that is, the Great Western, the Midland and the Bristol & Exeter. Brunel had seen no reason to keep to the 4-foot $8^1/_2$-inch gauge which George Stephenson adopted from the north of England tramroads, and for both comfort and goods-carrying favoured a 7-foot gauge for the Great Western routes. His broad gauge line from Bristol reached Gloucester in 1843 where it met the standard gauge line of the Birmingham and Gloucester Railway Company, which had followed the example set by the early railways in the north. The battle between the rival gauges raged for almost thirty years before the Great Western finally gave way, so that at Gloucester through passengers and goods had to change trains among the 'confusion of shouting out addresses of consignments, the chucking of packages across from truck to truck, the enquiries for missing articles, the loading, unloading, and reloading'.

At Temple Meads there was a more orderly scene, described in Morgan's *Guide* in 1849:

> A porter is ready to conduct you to the booking office, where you pay your fare and receive a ticket; you then ascend a flight of stairs to the platform. Having taken your place, and made all ready, you are now at ease to observe what is going on ... several engines with red hot fires in their bodies, and volumes of condensed steam issuing from them: one of them moves slowly towards you. The huge piece bellows at first like an elephant: deep, slow and terrific are the hoarse heavings that it makes. It is then linked to the carriages ... a whistle is sounded as a signal for starting—and you are off.

The construction of the routes was not achieved without difficulty or opposition. Charles Owen Cambridge of Whitminster declined to invest in the Great Western Railway, writing in 1834 that, 'I think it would not become me at 80 years of age to be dealing in adventurous speculations'. Landowners were not always willing to have a railway slicing through their lands, although none was so unyielding as Robert Gordon, the squire at Kemble, who only accepted the line from Swindon to Cheltenham after receiving substantial compensation and an undertaking that the railway would pass through his property by a totally unnecessary tunnel. Later Miss Anna Gordon wrote in 1883 that 'nothing shall induce me ever to give my consent to this proposed branch of the Swindon & Cheltenham Railway, having a *station* upon any of our land'.

Among the major engineering works in the county was the Mickleton tunnel where a dispute between the contractors was summarily settled by

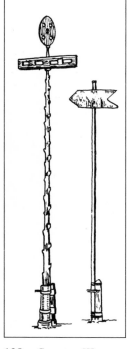

128 *Great Western Railway signals at Grange Court.*

XI *Tower of the University of Bristol.*

XII *Littledean House of Correction, built in 1791 as part of the reform of Gloucestershire prisons. Three others were built at Northleach, Horsley and Lawfords Gate (near Fishponds).*

XIII *Gloucester quay and docks by Edward Smith, 1878, showing the entrance from the river Severn.*

XIV *Royal Portbury Dock (foreground) and Avonmouth Docks. Beyond may be seen the second Severn Bridge, under construction in 1995, and the original Severn Bridge of 1966.*

Brunel gathering 2,000 of his own men to force his terms before peacekeeping troops could arrive from Coventry. The greatest engineering feat was the Severn tunnel, which was begun in 1873 but not finished until twelve years later. Underground springs flooded the workings and twice diver Lambert descended to close the emergency flood doors and save the incomplete tunnel. To this day powerful pumps work incessantly to keep the tunnel open.

The presence of a railway line had many lasting effects on the growth of 19th-century towns. At Gloucester there was a rapid enlargement of the built-up area near the stations, but Tewkesbury, which lacked a main line, stagnated. 'Whatever may be the ultimate effect of railroads it is evident that their introduction has hitherto been one of almost unmixed evil to the inhabitants of Tewkesbury', claimed a local writer in 1841. 'Of six and twenty stage coaches which, only twelve months ago, passed through this town every day to or from Worcester alone, not one conveyance of this kind now exists upon the road; nor is there even a single stage coach running through the place to Gloucester, though there were formerly nearly a score every day.' At Dursley Henry Vizard rightly forecast in 1839 that rail transport would have the effect of killing the local butter market formerly attended by dealers from Cheltenham and Stroud. On the other hand, during the agricultural depression of the 1880s the vicar of Rodmarton looked forward to the proposed line to Tetbury, for 'anything that seems likely to open up the country and give us fresh markets is to be welcomed'.

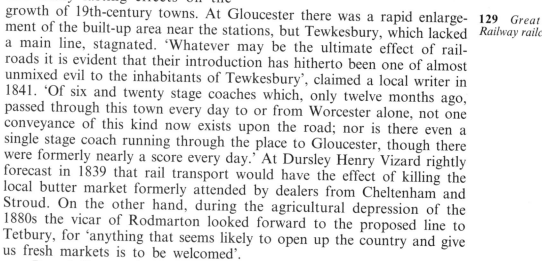

129 *Great Western Railway railcar at Ebley.*

Branch lines such as these spread a network throughout the county, and the innovation of 'rail-motors' on the Stonehouse to Chalford route in 1903 was extended to other rural branches. Though rarely profitable these local trains were often crowded, but as motor buses and cars reached the villages the train services declined. By 1965 when the Gloucester to Hereford line was closed, it was not unusual for the train to carry only one or two passengers, and today only the trunk routes and larger stations remain open.

24

Brunel in Bristol

Bristol gave Isambard K. Brunel his first engineering opportunity in 1829, when the Society of Merchant Venturers invited designs for a bridge to span the Avon Gorge at Clifton. Brunel entered the competition, but Thomas Telford, the judge, rejected his designs on the grounds that the spans were too great, and produced his own design. The committee then appointed four judges, who chose Brunel's plans, and so began this great engineer's connections with Bristol and the West Country. Work on the bridge was started in 1831, but owing to lack of funds the project was abandoned in 1854, and Brunel did not live to see the Clifton Suspension Bridge finished in 1864.

After the opening of the railway between London and Bristol, Brunel persuaded the directors of the Great Western Railway Company that Bristol must become a stage on the route to New York. When one of the directors complained of the excessive length of the railway line from London to Bristol, Brunel replied, 'Why not make it longer and have a steamboat to connect Bristol with New York, and call it the '*Great*

130 *Brunel's Clifton Suspension Bridge spanning the Avon Gorge.*

114

131 *Launch of SS Great Britain, 15 July 1843.*

Western'?' Through the influence of Richard Guppy, a man interested in shipping, the Great Western Steamship Company was formed and Brunel was appointed to design the new ship. She was built by William Patterson at Wapping Wharf in Bristol. She was a wooden paddle-wheel vessel, and the first steamship built as an Atlantic liner. The proposal attracted much ridicule, and one commentator remarked that 'they might as well talk of making a voyage from New York to the moon'. The *Great Western* confounded her critics, and in 1838 successfully completed her maiden voyage to New York in 15 days.

The next stage was to build a second ship, for a fortnightly service to America. In 1843 the *Great Britain* was launched. She was the first iron vessel and the first screw vessel. She was 322 feet long, 1,936 tons, with engines developing 1,000 h.p., and accommodation for 360 passengers. She was several hundred tons larger than any ship yet built and over 100 feet longer than any other ship. Amidst much rejoicing she sailed on 26 July 1845 on her first voyage to America—arriving in New York on 10 August. The *New York Herald* reported:

The monster of the deep, a sort of mastodon of this age, the *Great Britain*, arrived on Sunday afternoon, the 10th. She was telegraphed precisely at noon; the announcement threw the city into a state of great excitement and thousands rushed to the Battery, to the wharves on the East River, to the Brooklyn Heights, and to the Atlantic Steamship Pier at the foot of Clinton Street, to get a sight of her ... . This magnificent steamer came up the Bay in beautiful style ... . The great problem whether or not a steamer of the magnitude and construction of the *Great Britain*, and incorporating her principle of propulsion, could make a successful trip across the

132 *Bristol tram.*

ocean, is now satisfactorily and happily solved. The engines were never stopped until Captain Hosken had occasion to sound on Saint George's Bank.

In 1846 the *Great Britain* stranded in Dundrum Bay, northern Ireland and, although she was re-floated the next year, the Company was bankrupt. At the same time the *Great Western*, which had made 45 voyages on the New York run, was taken off service and laid up. In 1847 she was sold and ran on the West India mail route for 10 years before being broken up. The *Great Britain* was sold in 1850 and for 25 years ran between Liverpool and Australia, was afterwards converted into a sailing ship and then became a hulk off the Falkland Islands, used for the storing of wool and coal. It was expected that she would eventually break up, but in 1970 she returned to Bristol. In spite of the passage of time, the *Great Britain* has retained her unique hull form, a tribute to Brunel's engineering genius and to the skill and workmanship of Bristol ship-builders. On 19 July 1970, exactly 127 years later to the day, the *Great Britain* returned to the Bristol dock from which she was launched.

Just a hundred years ago, the government passed an act authorising the construction of tramways as vehicles of public transport. In doing so, it recognised the need felt not only in Bristol but in many other developing cities, which had grown in size with large numbers of people living in suburbs, for transport within the city. In August 1875, Bristol's first tramway service was begun, operated by the Bristol Tramway Company. These were horse trams, but it soon became obvious that some other means of propulsion was necessary in a city like Bristol built on hills. George White, who was the chief promoter of the Company, transformed the tramway system by converting it to electric traction.

As with the steamship and the locomotive, Bristol was foremost in the development of air transport. In 1910, Sir George White founded the Bristol Aeroplane Company which began the manufacture of aircraft only two years after Blériot's cross-Channel flight. In September of that year, a 'Bristol' boxkite became the first heavier-than-air aircraft to be used in British army manoeuvres. Through many years, the name of Bristol has been proudly borne by many aircraft—'Blenheims', 'Beauforts', 'Beaufighters' and the 'Britannia'. In 1949 the giant 'Brabazon' led the way for jumbo aircraft but for supersonic flight the works at Filton had to join with French Aerospatiale to produce 'Concorde' in 1969.

133 *Prototype 'Concorde' 002 on her maiden flight from Filton, 9 April 1969.*

25

The Port of Bristol

A glance at the map (p.119) will show immediately the many advantages of Bristol's position as a port. It lies near the head of one of England's four great estuaries—the Bristol Channel.

The first dock or harbour was developed at the confluence of the Avon and the Frome, some seven miles from the mouth of the River Avon, where the shipping was protected against storm and marauders. The town's wharves grew up along the Back on the south side of Bristol. As trade increased in the 13th century, these wharves near Bristol Bridge became so overcrowded that it was necessary to build new quays to accommodate the shipping. This was done by digging a new course for the River Frome and diverting it into the River Avon. It was a great engineering feat for the townsmen of those days to undertake. The seafaring ships were now able to reach the town on the north side and unload their rich cargoes of wine, woad and oil on the Broad and Narrow Quays. To the Back came ships from Wales and the southern coasts of England with their cargoes of fish, tin, hides and timber.

134 *Severn trow.*

At this time Bristol was more notable for shipping and distribution of goods than as a manufacturing centre, although cloth was being made in the town, mainly for the home market. During the 14th century cloth became Bristol's chief export, and by the close of the 15th century Bristol exported more cloth and imported more wine than any other provincial port.

When in 1373 the town was granted county status, the water boundaries of Bristol were extended to include the River Avon and the Bristol Channel as far as Steep Holm, and from there up to Denny Island and east to the mouth of the Avon, thus protecting the approaches to the harbour.

Off Portishead was the Kingroad where ships were able to wait for wind and tide, whilst three miles up the river was the Hungroad where vessels rested on the mud until the tide carried them up. Here some ships discharged their cargoes into smaller ships. At Pill nearby, pilots were available to bring ships up the river. The rise and fall of the tides and the tortuous course of the river practically prohibited vessels of any size coming up the river beyond the Hungroad.

As centuries passed nothing seems to have been done to improve the harbour further. No provision was made to keep a vessel afloat so that, as the tide ebbed, the ships settled down on the mud, and when they were

135 *Fairbairn crane, Bristol.*

heavily laden they sometimes settled awkwardly, running the risk of a broken back. The responsibility for maintaining the quays and for the development of small docks for ship building and repairing rested with the Corporation. Some merchants were content with their own private docks. Robert Aldworth, a sugar refiner, appears to have been the first to build a dock in 1626. When, however, the merchants began to demand better dock accommodation, the Corporation agreed to lease the quays to the Society of Merchant Venturers, who for nearly two hundred years maintained the port which was entirely within the city, and also made provisions for the safety of the shipping. By the 18th century, vessels exceeding 150 tons rarely came up the River Avon above the Hungroad. In 1712 a group of merchants constructed a dock at Sea Mills, which was the first mercantile dock to be built in England. A second dock, built by William Champion in 1765, was taken over by the Society of Merchant Venturers in 1770.

Apart from these two forward-looking exceptions the port remained a tidal one until 1803. Many schemes for converting the Avon into a dock were considered before one was finally accepted. In 1803 a company was formed to carry out William Jessop's plan for making a Floating Harbour so that the water would not drain away with every tide. About three miles of river, previously tidal in character, were formed into a dock unaffected by tidal ebb and flow, and a new channel for the tide was excavated on the south side of the city, called the New Cut. This cut enabled small craft from the Netham to enter the impounded harbour at Totterdown. The harbour thus created provided about 85 acres of dock space. Farther east a canal was built called the Feeder Canal which opened up a potential new industrial zone. It was a great improvement but did not in fact arrest the decline in trade for, in an attempt to regain the money laid out, excessive rates were charged by the Bristol Dock Company. It cost twice as much for a ship to dock at Bristol as it did at Liverpool and so the high charges levied drove trade to other ports. A Free Port Association was formed in 1846 and, as a result of continuous agitation by the Association and the Chamber of Commerce, the Bristol Dock Company sold the dock undertaking to the Corporation in 1848, who reduced the charges and so recaptured some of the trade.

It must not be assumed, however, that conditions at the port were alone responsible for the decline of Bristol's trade: the American war and the loss of the West India trade were only two factors which contributed to this state of affairs. Bristol, after all, had never been a centre which concentrated on a single industry and so the effect of the Industrial Revolution was hardly felt by comparison with the larger towns in the north. In some ways this was to her detriment for the merchants lost that sense of aggressive competition which for centuries had been their driving force. Some old industries such as sugar-refining and glass-making declined or disappeared altogether. With the need for machines, Bristol developed her engineering industries. The Bristol and Somerset coalfields enjoyed a period of prosperity, but the supplies were not in sufficient

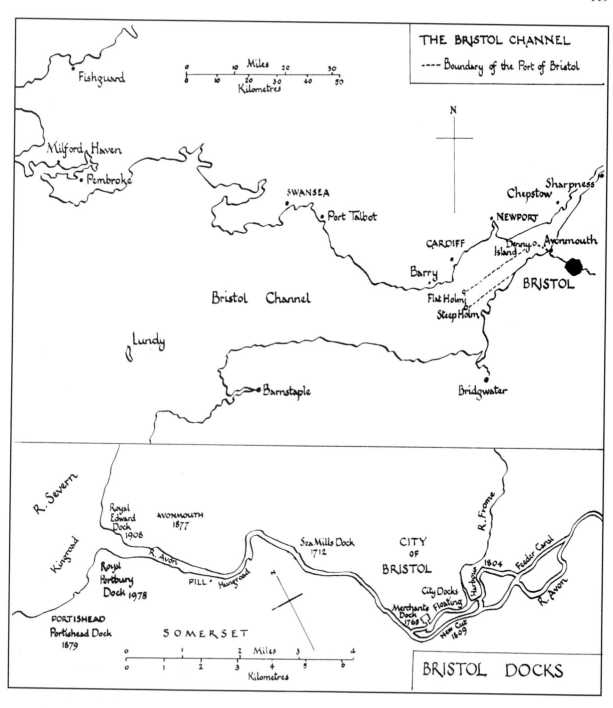

THE BRISTOL CHANNEL

---- Boundary of the Port of Bristol

Fishguard

Milford Haven

Pembroke

SWANSEA

Port Talbot

CARDIFF

Barry

Bristol Channel

Lundy

Barnstaple

N

Chepstow

Sharpness

NEWPORT

Denny o.
Island   Avonmouth

BRISTOL

Flat Holm

Steep Holm

Bridgwater

Miles

Kilometres

R. Severn

Royal
Edward
Dock
1908

AVONMOUTH
1877

R. Avon

Kingroad

Royal
Portbury
Dock 1978

PILL · Hungroad

Sea Mills Dock
1712

CITY
OF
BRISTOL

R. Frome

R. Avon

Feeder Canal

Harbour
1804

City Docks

Merchants Floating
Dock
1765

New Cut
1809

PORTISHEAD
Portishead Dock
1879

SOMERSET

N

Miles

Kilometres

BRISTOL DOCKS

quantity to attract large industries. And, as time went on, many vessels
became too large to navigate the Avon easily and a new harbour was
needed at the mouth of the river. In 1877 the first river mouth dock was
made at Avonmouth. Two years later Portishead dock on the south side

136 *Bristol Docks.*

137 *Old lighthouse, Avonmouth.*

was added. They were private undertakings and for a few years Bristol had three ports, each competing with the other for the city's trade. Obviously this state of affairs could not be allowed to continue. In 1884 the Corporation purchased the river mouth docks and so secured control of the whole of the facilities of the port of Bristol. Now at last a new and fruitful period in the development of the port began. In 1908 the Royal Edward dock with a lock 875 feet long and 100 feet wide, capable of berthing the largest vessels afloat, was opened and subsequently the accommodation has been enlarged on several occasions.

When the Corporation acquired the Avonmouth and Portishead docks in 1884, the foreign imports amounted to only 820,000 tons and the total tonnage of incoming ships was 1,247,000 tons. By 1972 about 1,800 vessels with a tonnage of four millions entered the port of Bristol each year from overseas countries. A road known as the Portway provides for transport between the river mouth docks, the city and the great arterial roads of the country. The expansion of trade led to the setting up of new industries, such as the manufacture of paper, animal feeding stuffs, fertilisers, the smelting of zinc and the production of aircraft and aero engines. After the Second World War, it became evident that a more extensive dock was necessary at the mouth of the River Avon and that the docks at Avonmouth were not adequate. In August 1978 the Royal Portbury Dock was completed just across the River Avon from the existing docks. This new dock is able to accommodate ships of 70,000 tons.

In 1991 a private company owned by Devereux Mordaunt and David Ord acquired the port of Bristol from Bristol City Council after a public ownership of 143 years. By 1995 cargo traffic had increased by 2,000,000 tons and 5 per cent in revenue.

26

Parliamentary Reform

In Parliament the county had been represented by two Members since at least 1283, while Bristol and Gloucester sent Members from 1295. The county Members were usually Gloucestershire gentry among whom the Berkeley family feature most often. In the 18th and early 19th centuries there was a strong division between supporters of the two great families, the Tory Beauforts and the Whig Berkeleys. In common with other counties Gloucestershire had experienced no election contest for many years, the parties nominating one Member each, until 1776 when George Berkeley, then 23 years old, challenged William Bromley Chester for the vacant seat previously held by a Tory. Polling continued for 11 days with both candidates spending enormous sums to bring in voters from far out of the county. According to Lord North some years later, when supporting a Government grant towards Chester's expenses, 'Mr. Chester in the great contest for Gloucestershire had, as it is said, spent from £20,000 to £30,000, but nevertheless left at his death from £3,000 to £4,000 unpaid'. Some estimates put the total cost of the battle to both parties at £100,000, and one result was that both the Duke of Beaufort and the Berkeley family were so financially exhausted that, as John Parsons of Kemerton was told by a correspondent, 'His Grace and Lord Berkeley have settled the peace of the county of Gloucester, as far as in their power, by mutually agreeing One and One'. The truce lasted until 1811. By the Reform Acts of 1832 and 1885 the county was divided first into two and then into four divisions.

The cities preferred to elect their own leading citizens unless influenced by the parties to choose neighbouring gentry or even nationally known politicians. Gloucester was traditionally Whig in outlook and the corporation were quite prepared to create freemen who would vote that way in a forthcoming election; in 1789, for example, 425 were added to the roll. However, money rather than political views was the decisive factor. In 1830 John Phillpotts was elected with 814 votes, many of them from Gloucester citizens living in Birmingham and London, but having little money left to repeat this expensive exercise in 1831 he secured only 270 votes and lost his seat. Evidence of bribery of nearly 2,000 voters preceded the loss of one of Gloucester's two Members in 1885, and similar charges were upheld in Gloucester in 1859 and in Cheltenham in 1847. The latter was a Berkeley stronghold from 1832 to 1865, when

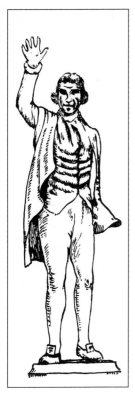

138 *Edmund Burke's statue, Bristol.*

Colonel Francis Berkeley was narrowly defeated in a wild election in which one of his supporters was shot dead in the High Street by an over-excited Conservative.

In Bristol a political crisis arose in 1774. An election was imminent and the retiring members of Parliament were Lord Clare and Matthew Brickdale. Both were unpopular with the merchants, having voted steadily for an anti-American policy. The Whigs therefore invited Henry Cruger, an American merchant who had considerable interests in both New York and Bristol, and Edmund Burke to stand as members of Parliament for the city. At the time England was drifting into war with the Colonies and the Bristol merchants, heavily hit in their colonial trade, wanted peace. After one of the most exciting elections to take place in Bristol, Burke and Cruger were elected. The successful candidates were chaired, bells rung, and cannons fired. After six years of service as their representative Bristol people became dissatisfied with Burke's representation of the city. In his farewell speech, declining election in 1780, he invited the electors of Bristol to consider 'what shadows we are, and what shadows we pursue'. These words fell on empty ears, and yet there was something prophetic in Burke's utterance, for indeed the greatest days for Bristol were over, for the war with the American colonies had struck a great blow at Bristol's trade.

A new crisis accompanied by rioting developed during the campaign for the Reform Bill in 1831. The 19th-century middle classes and their leaders knew that their only hope of making their influence felt in Parliament was by having the right to vote. It was believed that not only did far too few people have a vote, but also that the wrong places were returning members to Parliament. By 1830 the idea of parliamentary reform had gripped the people's imagination and the Reform Bill of 1831 excited much interest in Bristol. Large meetings were held by both political parties, and petitions in favour of reform were sent to Parliament.

In the spring of 1831 Lord John Russell introduced his Reform Bill but it was rejected. Later in the year another Bill, introduced by Lord Grey, passed the Commons, but Sir Charles Wetherell, Recorder of Bristol, strongly opposed it, saying 'that the reform fever had a great deal abated in Bristol'. This was far from true and his statement provoked great feeling in the city. When the Bill went to the House of Lords, the bishop of Bristol was one of the most prominent opponents. So unpopular was Sir Charles Wetherell that, when it was known that he was coming to open the assizes in Bristol, the mob resolved to give him a rousing reception. The mayor, worried by the situation, sought help from the government and reluctantly Lord Melbourne promised to send troops, who were only to be employed in the gravest emergency. The total strength of the cavalry was such that the number was totally inadequate either to overawe the people or keep the peace. A large number of special constables were sworn in. It is probable that the preparations made for the safe conduct of the Recorder into the city may have provoked the mob to violence. When Sir Charles arrived in Bristol, he was received with

| 1300 |
| GLOUCESTER 2 |
| GLOUCESTERSHIRE 2 |
| BRISTOL 2 |

| 1832 |
| TEWKESBURY 2 |
| CHELTENHAM 1 |
| GLOUCESTER 2 |
| STROUD 2   CIRENCESTER 1 |
| GLOUCESTERSHIRE 4 |
| BRISTOL 2 |

| 1885 |
| CHELTENHAM 1 |
| GLOUCESTER 1 |
| GLOUCESTERSHIRE 5 |
| Miles 0 10 20 |
| BRISTOL 4 |

PARLIAMENTARY REPRESENTATION

The number of M.P's for Bristol was increased to 5 in 1918 and 6 in 1949.

Since 1918 Gloucestershire has had 4 M.P's and Gloucester and Cheltenham one each.

One county constituency went to Avon in 1974.

139 *Parliamentary representation.*

hisses and his carriage pelted with stones, but he reached the Guildhall in safety. Having opened the assizes with violent interruptions, he retired to the Mansion House where he was met with howls of derision. So hostile was the mob that Sir Charles Wetherell considered it advisable to make his escape and did so in disguise over the roofs of the buildings. By midnight he had left the city.

Scenes of destruction followed: the Mansion House was fired and looted, together with the Customs House and other houses in Queen Square. The troops were called in, the Riot Act read, but Colonel Brereton refused to fire on the mobs, anxious to avoid bloodshed if possible, and his leniency was taken as a sign of weakness. The rioters, now drunk by the wine which they had taken from the cellars of the Mansion House, sought fresh fields of destruction.

The next day the rioting continued with the firing of the gaols, and the destruction of the Bishop's Palace. For three days the riots continued, and so great was the fire that it is said that the reflection in the sky

140 *Burning of the Bishop's Palace, Bristol during the Reform Bill riots, 1831. After the burning of the three prisons, the rioters turned on the house of the Bishop, who had voted against the Bill. Painting by W.J. Muller, 1831.*

141 *Lawford's Gate prison.*

could be seen at Cardiff. Charles Kingsley, who was a schoolboy in Bristol at the time, described the scene as being like Dante's Inferno. Reinforcements of troops eventually quelled the rioters and peace reigned once more. The mayor was tried for neglect, but acquitted. Colonel Brereton was court martialled, a few of the mob were hanged and many others were sentenced to transportation. So ended the most famous riots in the city's history. Lord Palmerston recorded in his diary, 'There has been a tremendous row in Bristol. All the public buildings of the town have been burnt, besides many private houses, and three hundred of the mob killed or wounded by the sabres of the cavalry'.

In 1832 the Reform Bill became law. One of the first acts of the reformed Parliament was to appoint a Royal Commission to examine and report on local conditions. It was clear that the dissatisfaction at the way in which local affairs were being managed in Bristol was largely responsible for the riots. As a result of the investigations, the Municipal Corporations Act of 1835 was passed which revolutionised the system of local government. At first, the chief functions of the newly elected Council were the lighting and watching of the borough, but by later Acts of Parliament these functions were extended until they covered every branch of local welfare. And so began our modern system of city management.

27

Law and Order

From the time of the Middle Ages the monarch administered justice through his itinerant judges holding assizes. The chief royal official residing in each county was the sheriff, whose duties in carrying out the king's commands were arduous and sometimes dangerous. As late as 1631 the sheriff personally led his constables in arresting John Skinnington, an agitator against inclosures, only to be vigorously opposed by a hostile crowd in the Forest of Dean and forced to withdraw.

The sheriff was assisted in his work by the Justices of the Peace, whose judicial office had been fully established by statute in 1361. They were empowered to judge almost every kind of misdemeanour, and from 1362 they met four times a year in quarter sessions. It was the inconvenience for Bristolians to seek justice at either Gloucester or Ilchester (then the county town of Somerset) that led the citizens to seek the great charter of liberties in 1373, raising the city to the status of a county

142 *The Lord Mayor of Bristol's coach, Victoria Rooms, Bristol.*

143 *Old county gaol, Gloucester.*

entitled to its own assizes. Bristol had the additional privilege that the mayor and sheriff, and from 1499 the aldermen also, were automatically Justices and not appointed by the Crown, as was usual. This procedure continued until 1835. Both assizes and quarter sessions were replaced in 1972 by new courts sitting more frequently.

Bringing offenders before the magistrates depended upon the activity of law-abiding citizens or informers and the somewhat ineffective parish constables, perhaps reinforced by special constables. On occasions of serious disorder there was no alternative to calling out the troops. Although the Bristol riots of 1831 was the most famous occasion, it was not the first time, nor the last, that the army and local yeomanry were mobilised. James Wolfe, the conqueror of Quebec, experienced his first independent command not against foreign enemies of the realm but the poor weavers of the Stroud valleys in 1756. Later, troops were prudently stationed in Dursley during the Chartist unrest in 1839. The high price of bread in the late 18th century provoked the colliers of both the Forest of Dean and Kingswood to rioting, and in 1793 protests arose in Bristol over the payment of tolls to cross Bristol bridge. The authorities had promised that tolls would not be collected after September 1793, but in spite of the promise tolls were advertised. A mob gathered near the bridge, burnt the toll gates, and greeted the magistrates and a body of soldiers, summoned to enforce order, with a shower of stones. The soldiers were ordered to clear the bridge and fired on the mob, killing and wounding many of the rioters.

Such extreme measures could not normally be taken. In place of adequate police the chief deterrent against crime was the excessive penalty for those found guilty. In 1741, for example, Frances Griffith of Bristol was sentenced to be hanged for stealing goods worth £8, and in 1831 William Morgan, a 15-year-old boy, was sentenced to 14 years' transportation for stealing an umbrella. It is only fair to add that in the same year most of the farm labourers who joined the 'Swing' riots against the introduction of threshing machinery around Tetbury were treated with leniency.

The most extensive and notorious company of thieves, highway robbers and extortioners was the Cock Road Gang of Bitton and Kingswood. They flourished from at least 1780. The *Tennis Court* inn at Warmley was one meeting place of the gang members, who also attended the annual Lansdown fair outside Bath to extort protection money from local farmers. Despite the many Bitton men and women who were hanged and transported, leading one judge to remark with heavy humour, 'I thought I had hanged the whole of that parish long ago', the gang was still in existence in 1828. Crime and petty offences increased six- or seven-fold between 1805 and 1836 especially near Bristol, well above national rates. It was with these conditions in mind, coupled with the unemployment and unrest around Stroud, that the county magistrates in 1839 became the first in the country to adopt Peel's Act for establishing a police force.

144 *Gloucester county gaol, 'a model for all England' built in 1791.*

In a related sphere the Gloucestershire Justices were even greater pioneers, for they made the county's prisons 'a model for all England'. This was the achievement of Sir George Onesiphorus Paul (1746-1820), the son of a successful Woodchester clothier, who as sheriff in 1780 discovered the appalling conditions in Gloucester Castle gaol.

> The whole herd of Prisoners, those committed for trial and those convicted, the young and the old offender, are indiscriminately driven at night into one dark pen ... . A ponderous chain crosses this place of rest, and, passing the middle link of each man's fetter, it is made fast at each end, and the whole number are threaded together ... . Enlarged from these horrors of the night, this entire indiscriminate number of prisoners are crouded into one room, 12 feet by 11; so that there being now 65 prisoners, each man has a space of less than two square feet to stand in.

One out of four could expect to die of gaol fever or smallpox.

After ten years' campaign a new county gaol and four houses of correction were opened in 1791, in which Paul's ideas were put into practice. The types of prisoners were segregated, and work was provided. All the prisoners received a good daily main meal, fresh air and exercise, heated accommodation, preferably with separate day and night cells, and the prisoners were supervised by salaried staff. The 1791 Prisons Act and buildings throughout the country were based on the Gloucestershire reforms, while Paul went on to turn his attention to another scandal, the awful plight of the mentally ill. After many delays the County Lunatic Asylum, one of the first in the country, was opened in 1823.

The year 1597 stands out in the history of the Justices for the imposition of the heaviest burden of administrative work that ever fell upon them—the control of the Poor Law. Later statutes enlarged and amended this Act, but the principles remained the same. Each parish was responsible for its own poor, and could levy a rate for their relief (the origin of our local tax arrangements today), the whole system being supervised by the magistrates. In Bristol it was different, for in 1696 John Cary put forward a proposal to establish a better and more equitable system of dealing with the destitute poor. His idea was that every able-bodied person would be compelled to work, the infirm would be cared for and the young adequately trained. A body called the Corporation of the Poor, comprising the mayor, aldermen and 48 elected representatives of the 12 city wards was established. About 300 persons were under its care by 1700.

In the county from about 1770 expenditure on poor relief generally increased rapidly. Mitcheldean is typical. With a population of less than six hundred and only about one hundred ratepayers, the cost of relief rose from about £50 in the mid-18th century to a peak of £546 in 1800.

A growing national population, poor harvests, and wartime conditions contributed to the crisis, and it is not surprising that parish overseers of the poor should sometimes have reacted harshly. It became the practice to remove poor people from a parish unless they could prove that it was their legal place of settlement, and real hardship might arise. In 1746 a Gloucester girl, Ann Newman, married a Welsh soldier stationed in the town. She stayed behind at home when his regiment moved; but when she applied for assistance the poor girl was abruptly packed off to Aberystwyth, a place which she had probably never even heard of, because that was her husband's legal dwelling place. Similarly, pauper children were apprenticed away from their homes lest they too might become a burden on the rates, and some unfortunate ones were thrust into factories like the three Andrews boys from Mitcheldean, sent to Kidderminster carpet works between 1807 and 1810. Gloucestershire magistrates in 1795 adopted the Berkshire 'Speenhamland system', by which the rate of relief was adjusted

145 *Young Kingswood miners in their working clothes with dagger candlesticks and tallow dips, 1833. 'By the breaking in of the water at Kingswood Lodge Coalpit these five boys were shut in for six nights and days entirely destitute of food.' Money from this engraving was to be spent on apprenticing the boys to a safer trade.*

Berkshire 'Speenhamland system', by which the rate of relief was adjusted according to the price of bread and wages of the applicant. This well-intentioned plan had the unfortunate result of perpetuating low wages and discouraging a man from working harder.

Workhouses were built in the towns and many villages, so that there should be some income from the spinning and pinmaking done by the inmates. Among other methods of reducing the cost of poor relief was the reform of the Uley workhouse devised in the 1830s by T.J. Lloyd Baker of Hardwicke (1777-1841), whose son T.B. Lloyd Baker (1807-86) was a founder of the reformatory school idea in 1852. His stricter administration of relief, like that of the Corporation of the Poor in Bristol, foreshadowed the Poor Law Reform Act of 1834. By setting up new Boards of Guardians responsible for Union workhouses serving a group of parishes, this Act at last removed from the Justices and local parish officials the burdensome responsibility of social welfare.

28

The Twentieth Century

There are people living today who can remember greater changes in their lifetime than had occurred for centuries. Their childhood memories seem as remote to their grandchildren as many of the events described in earlier chapters. About 1900 a farm labourer in Woolstone earned 12s. 6d. [62^1/$_2$p] a week, and his wife spent 2s. 6d. of it in doing the whole week's shopping in Cheltenham, four miles on foot, by train from the little railway station at Gotherington or by the carrier's cart. The 19th-century innovations of the oil lamp and gas light, so welcome to an older generation, were still in widespread use. Before 1929 the county 'was sparsely supplied with electricity' and even fifty years ago half the rural area had none—no electric light or power, television, refrigerators or vacuum cleaners. It seems no less extraordinary that in 1914 in all Gloucestershire there were only 1,797 cars and 28 lorries; in the smaller county of Gloucestershire in 1991 residents had 236,297 cars and more households (30 per cent) had two or more than those (24 per cent) which had none. The beginning of the village bus service is often cited as the single most important change in the countryside before the Second World War, but since 1950 the spreading personal ownership of cars has almost entirely killed off rural public transport.

147 *Yate.*

148 *Lechlade market place, c.1925. The fleet of local buses, 'the single most important change in the countryside' in the early 20th century.*

130

149 *The growth of Bristol, 1900-1970.*

Early in the century the population of the countryside was declining, partly due to the farming depression followed by the premature death of so many men whose names are recorded on 1914-18 war memorials. The 20th-century wars, however, also had the effect of reviving farming fortunes with a return to arable husbandry, although the agricultural labour force has continued to diminish and with it the number of village shops, post offices, schools and chapels. But better communications by the motorways and the Severn Bridge, faster trains from Bristol Parkway and the east Cotswolds, together with the attractions of much of the county for retirement, second homes and the tourist trade, have brought in a new population which has revitalised a much altered rural lifestyle. Conservation and tourist interests have helped to preserve old Gloucestershire farming specialities which had almost disappeared, like the Cots-

150 *Berkeley atomic power station.*

151 *The Severn Bridge replaced in 1966 the last and probably the oldest regular ferry across the river between Aust and Beachley.*

wold breed of sheep, the making of farmhouse Gloucester cheese which had ceased almost entirely by 1919, cider-making which declined in the 1920s and the Gloucestershire breed of cattle which had been nearly wiped out by foot-and-mouth disease. The changing character of the county has also been affected by the virtual extinction of the traditional industries of cloth manufacture in the Stroud valleys and mining north of Bristol and in the Forest of Dean, where there was much hardship during the depression of the 1920s and 1930s.

In contrast to the declining population of the remote countryside, there has been a vast increase in the size of the principal towns, and in the 1970s and 1980s the county's population of Bristol had by 1900 risen to 328,800, partly due to an expansion of the city boundaries, reaching a peak of 445,000 in 1955. More and more houses were necessary to accommodate the growing city, which stretched out into south Gloucestershire and north Somerset. As the city invaded the countryside the need of open spaces was soon recognised, and now the people of Bristol enjoy some 3,000 acres of fine open downs and parks.

Whilst the Second World War caused irreparable damage and much that was irreplaceable was lost, it did provide an opportunity for replanning many parts of the city. The destruction of 3,000 homes with the partial destruction of another 90,000 led to the development of new suburbs. In fact, a new Bristol has risen from the ruins of the old. By 1961 Bristol and the adjacent urban areas in Gloucestershire had a population of over half a million people, a figure which in 1991 had risen to nearly 600,000, a little over half that of the whole area of the city and old county. The industrial growth of this southern part of the county accelerated in the 1960s. The world's first commercial nuclear power station was opened at Berkeley in 1962, followed by another at Oldbury-on-Severn in 1968, and vast chemical works near Avonmouth in 1962-3. A new town was started in 1966 at Yate. The junction of the London-South Wales M4 and Birmingham to Exeter M5 motorways at Almondsbury attracted distributive and other industries in the 1970s and 1980s, among which the Aztec technical park of the mid-1980s was noteworthy. The M4 motorway was itself distinguished by the outstanding engineering achievement of the Severn crossing, the first bridge being opened in 1966 and the second in 1996.

Northwards the M5 motorway shortens the distance to the other main urban area of the county. Gloucester and Cheltenham have grown less dramatically than Bris-

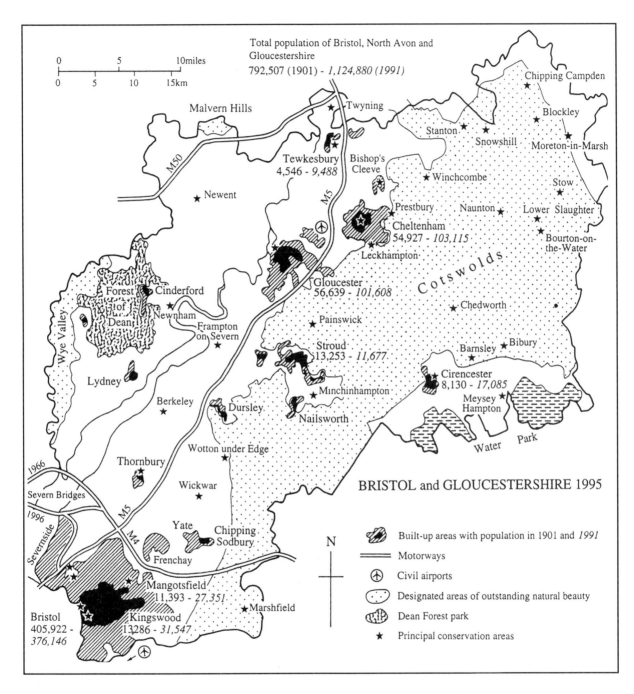

Total population of Bristol, North Avon and Gloucestershire
792,507 (1901) - *1,124,880 (1991)*

Chipping Campden

Malvern Hills

Blockley

Twyning

Stanton

Snowshill

Moreton-in-Marsh

Tewkesbury
4,546 - *9,488*

Bishop's Cleeve

Winchcombe

Stow

Newent

Prestbury

Naunton

Lower Slaughter

Cheltenham
54,927 - *103,115*

Leckhampton

Bourton-on-
the-Water

C o t s w o l d s

Forest of Dean

Cinderford

Gloucester
56,639 - *101,608*

Newnham

Chedworth

Frampton on Severn

Painswick

Wye Valley

Lydney

Stroud
13,253 - *11,677*

Barnsley

Bibury

Berkeley

Dursley

Minchinhampton

Cirencester
8,130 - *17,085*

Nailsworth

Meysey Hampton

Wotton under Edge

Water   Park

Thornbury

BRISTOL and GLOUCESTERSHIRE 1995

Wickwar

1966

Severn Bridges

Yate

Chipping Sodbury

N

1996

Frenchay

Severnside

Mangotsfield
11,393 - *27,351*

Marshfield

Bristol
405,922 -
376,146

Kingswood
13286 - *31,547*

Built-up areas with population in 1901 and *1991*

Motorways

Civil airports

Designated areas of outstanding natural beauty

Dean Forest park

Principal conservation areas

tol, but the two towns and adjacent suburbs are now only separated by a narrow belt of fields, and in 1991 had a combined population of about 208,300. Gloucester in the present century has seen the rise and fall of the Gloucester Aircraft Company where such notable aircraft as the 'Gladiator' and 'Meteor' were made. The works closed in 1960, to be followed into

152 *Bristol   and Gloucestershire, 1995.*

153 A 'Gladiator' over Gloucestershire: one of the most successful aircraft built at Gloucester.

followed into oblivion or takeover by other long-familiar factories, such as Morelands match factory (1976) and the Gloucester Wagon Works (mid-1980s) in Gloucester and Sir George Dowty's group of aircraft and other works in and around Cheltenham. The manufacture of precision machinery and instruments remains an important feature of mid-Gloucestershire but in 1995 the service industries everywhere accounted for much employment, for instance at the Government Communications Headquarters at Cheltenham, the regional offices of government departments in Bristol, the electricity generating board at Gloucester and the headquarter offices of local authorities, insurance companies and building societies.

The enlargement and rebuilding of the towns, and other forms of 20th-century development, caused the loss of many fine historic landmarks. Historians can only deplore the ruthless destruction of ancient buildings of architectural merit in Bristol, Gloucester and Tewkesbury. Old photographs of Bristol show that the 1941-2 blitz was by no means solely responsible for such vandalism. The abstract ideal of preserving England's heritage, so strongly held during the blitz years, was embodied in post-war planning legislation. Its effectiveness may be judged, however, by the fact that in Gloucester, of 339 buildings thought worthy of protection under the Town and Country Planning Act of 1947, only 185 remained in 1971. There have, of course, been many positive achieve-

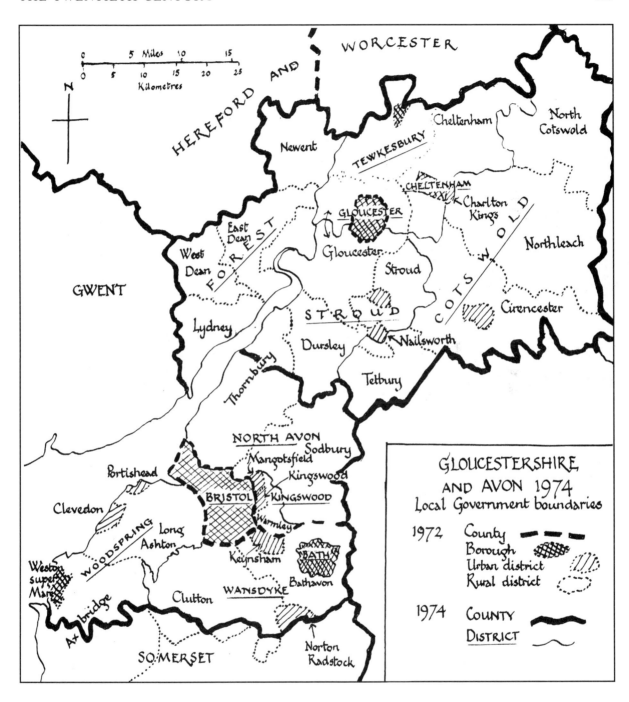

154 *Gloucestershire and Avon, 1974.*

the Cotswold water park and the two designated areas of outstanding natural beauty in the Cotswolds and Wye Valley, though the effects of regulation and tourism now pose new threats. Private individuals have also contributed. Sir Philip Stott restored the village of Stanton between 1906 and

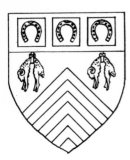

155 *Gloucestershire County Council arms.*

1925, and the Bristol and Gloucestershire Archaeological Society formed a trust to care for Arlington Row at Bibury from 1928 to 1949. More recently the Bristol Civic Society led the opposition in 1969 to the closure of the City Docks, which provide so much of the maritime character of the city centre.

The rapid growth of the major towns with industries in no way dependent upon local sources of raw materials may have accentuated the natural division between town and country, but the late Victorian local government reform did little to diminish it. The Municipal Corporation Act of 1835 had improved the archaic constitutions of towns like Gloucester and Tewkesbury, whilst the Municipal Corporations Act of 1883 deprived small towns like Berkeley and Thornbury of their borough status. A few years later in 1888 the County Council was established to administer the whole rural area in place of the many functions of the magistrates, with some powers exercised by the district and parish councils created by a further Act in 1894. After the Second World War educational, planning and social welfare services multiplied, eventually bringing about the first major reform of local administration since the 1890s. In 1974 local government was reconstructed under an Act passed two years previously. The administrative map of the old counties and district councils, including the city of Bristol and the county boroughs, was wiped clean. A new county of Avon was created. This was divided into six new district councils of which Bristol, Kingswood and Northavon (being the southern part of Gloucestershire) were three. The reform was expensive, unpopular and unsatisfactory, leading to a further reorganisation under the Local Government Act of 1992 by which Avon County Council was abolished in 1996. Bristol became a unitary authority, in effect recovering its pre-1974 status, and the former south Gloucestershire parts of Kingswood and Northavon because another; the rest of Gloucestershire retained a two-tier system of county and district councils.

A thousand years ago the shires were being formed. Gloucestershire then came to contain Bristol, the place at the bridge on the north bank of the Avon, but at first neither the Forest of Dean nor independent Winchcombeshire. Now, after all the intervening events recorded here which have moulded their character, the great seaport city of Bristol and the ancient county of Gloucestershire enter the new millennium in the same clearly recognisable shape.

Bibliography

This bibliography is a guide to further reading about the history of Bristol and Gloucestershire. It is not a list of the works consulted in the writing of this book. It is also not a catalogue of learned and scholarly studies of interest only to the specialist. However, before making suggestions about further reading, a few important reference books must be mentioned.

Chiefly for Reference

There are short and straightforward guides to all local historical sources relating to Gloucestershire in libraries, record offices and museums in B.S. Smith's *Gloucestershire Local History Handbook* (2nd edn. 1975) and *Avon Local History Handbook*, ed. J.S. Moore (1979).

The *Catalogue of the Gloucestershire Collection in Gloucester Public Library* (1928) lists almost every Gloucestershire book and pamphlet written before 1928, and this remarkably fine collection is well kept up-to-date. Among the many books that have been published on Gloucestershire there are a few really important ones, the titles of which should become familiar to all readers of this book. They are:

The Victoria History of the County of Gloucestershire. In progress, eight volumes published. Eventually it will cover all the old county, and the city of Bristol.

S. Rudder, *A New History of Gloucestershire* (1779, reprinted 1977)

R. Atkyns, *The Ancient and Present State of Glocestershire* [sic] (1712, reprinted 1974)

The *Transactions* of the Bristol and Gloucestershire Archaeological Society (annual volumes from 1876).

Bristol Record Society *Publications* (1930 to date)

These last two series are mentioned here chiefly because they contain the results of some of the latest research on the history of Bristol and Gloucestershire.

Finally, there are nowadays other sources of expert advice on local history matters. The reference libraries of Bristol, Gloucester and Cheltenham, and some library branches contain collections of local history books. The Bristol Record Office and Gloucestershire Record Office are the repositories of local archives. There are museums open daily throughout the year at Bristol, Gloucester, Cheltenham, Cirencester, Stroud, Northleach and Lower Soudley. And throughout the region local historical societies and adult education organisations hold meetings which bring together people interested in local history.

A Guide to the Industrial Archaeology of Gloucestershire (1992)

Aston, M. and Iles, R., *The Archaeology of Avon* (1987)

Bird, W.H., *Old Gloucestershire Churches* (1928)

Brown, H.G. and Harris, P.J., *Bristol, England* (1964)

Buchanan, R.A. and Cossens, N., *The Industrial Archaeology of the Bristol Region* (1969)

Burrough, T.H.B., *Bristol* [City Building Series] (1970)

Carus-Wilson, E.M., *Medieval Merchant Venturers* (1954)

Comino, M., *Gimson and the Barnsleys* (1980)

Collins, N.R., Downs, R.A. and Pullan, R.H., *North Gloucestershire Sub-Regional Study* (1970)

Darby, H.C. and Terrett, I.B., *Domesday Geography of Midland England* (1954)

Darvill, T., *Prehistoric Gloucestershire* (1987)

Finberg, H.P.R., *Gloucestershire: an Illustrated Essay on the History of the Landscape* (1955)

Finberg, H.P.R., ed., *Gloucestershire Studies* (1957)

Fullbrook-Leggatt, L.E.W.O., *Anglo-Saxon and Medieval Gloucester* (1952)

Gloucestershire Federation of Women's Institutes, *I Remember: Social Life in Gloucestershire Villages, 1850-1950* (1965)

Gomme, A., Jenner, M. and Little, B., *Bristol: an Architectural History* (1979)

Greenacre, F. and Stondard, S., *Bristol, the Landscape* (1986)

Hadfield, C., *Canals of South and South East England* (1969), *Canals of South Wales and the Border* (1967)

Hart, C.E., *The Free Miners* (1953), *Royal Forest* (1966), *The Industrial History of Dean* (1971)

Hart, G., *History of Cheltenham* (1965)

Heighwey, C., *Anglo-Saxon Gloucestershire* (1987)

Hilton, R.H., *A Medieval Society*, (1967)

Household, H., *Thames and Severn Canal* (1969)

Jones, A., *The Cotswolds* (1994)

Jurica, John, *Gloucester: A Pictorial History* (1994)

Latimer, J., *Annals of Bristol, Sixteenth to Nineteenth Centuries*, 4 vols. (1887-1900)

Little, B., *The City and County of Bristol* (1954)

MacDermott, E.T., (revised by C.R. Clinker), *History of the Great Western Railway*, 3 vols. (1964)

MacInnes, C.M., *Bristol: a Gateway of Empire* (1968)

MacInnes, C.M. and Whittard, W.F., ed., *Bristol and its adjoining Counties* (1955)

Mann, J. de L., *The Cloth Industry in the West of England from 1640 to 1880* (1971)

Mansfield, R.J., *Forest Story* (1964)

Marshall, W., *The Rural Economy of Gloucestershire*, 2 vols. (1789)

McGrath, P., *The Merchant Venturers of Bristol* (1975)

McWhirr, A., *Roman Gloucestershire* (1981)

Moir, E., *Local Government in Gloucestershire, 1775-1800* (1969)

Mowl, T., *To build the Second City, Architects and Craftsmen of Georgian Bristol* (1991)

Neale, W.G., *Port of Bristol, 1848-1899*, Vol. I (1968), Vol. II (1970)

Payne, G.E., *Gloucestershire, a Physical, Social and Economic Survey and Plan* (1947)

Pevsner, N., *Buildings of England: North Somerset and Bristol* (1958)

Platts, A. and Hainton, G.H., *Education in Gloucestershire* (1954)

Ralph, E., *The Great White Book of Bristol*, Bristol Record Society, vol.32 (1979)

Smith, A.H., *Place-names of Gloucestershire* (1964-5), 4 vols., especially its Introduction in vol.IV.

Tann, J., *Gloucestershire Woollen Mills* (1967)

Vanes, J., *Overseas Trade of Bristol in the Sixteenth Century*, Bristol Record Society, vol.31 (1978)

Verey, D.C.W., *Buildings of England: Gloucestershire*, 2 vols. (1970, under revision 1995)

Welch, F.B.A. and Crookall, R., *British Regional Geology: Bristol and Gloucester District* (2nd edn. 1949)

Whitefield, G., *Journals* (1960)

Whiting, J.R.S., *Prison Reform in Gloucestershire, 1776-1820* (1975)

Willcox, W.B., *Gloucestershire, 1590-1640* (1940)

Winstone, R., Illustrated books on Bristol, with photographs of street scenes, buildings, etc., from 1850, 14 vols. (1958-69)

The Bristol Branch of the Historical Association has published 85 pamphlets, including:

Bettey, J.H., *Bristol Parish Churches during the Reformation, c.1530-1560* (1979)

Bettey, J.H., *Suppression of the Religious Houses in Bristol* (1990)

Bettey, J.H., *Bristol Cathedral, the Rebuilding of the Nave* (1993)

Branigan, K., *The Romans in the Bristol Area* (1969)

Buchanan, R.A., *Nineteenth-century engineers in the port of Bristol* (1970)

Burgess, C,. *The Parish Church and the Laity in Medieval Bristol* (1992)

Butcher, E.E., *Bristol Corporation of the Poor* (1972)

Cannon, John, *The Chartists in Bristol* (1964)

Carus-Wilson, E.M., *The Merchant Adventurers of Bristol in the Fifteenth Century* (1962)

Cobb, P.G., *The Oxford Movement in Nineteenth Century Bristol* (1988)

Farr, G., *The Steamship Great Western* (1963)

Farr, G., *The Steamship Great Britain* (1965)

Farr, G., *Bristol Shipbuilding in the Nineteenth Century* (1971)

Grinsell, L.V., *Prehistoric Bristol* (1969)

Harvey, C. and Press, J., *Sir George White of Bristol* (1989)

Lamb, P.G., *Electricity in Bristol, 1863-1948* (1981)

Large, D. and Round, Frances, *Public Health in Mid-Victorian Bristol* (1974)

McGrath, Patrick, *John Whitson and the Merchant Community of Bristol* (1970)

McGrath, Patrick, *Bristol and the Civil War* (1981)

MacInnes, C.M., *Bristol and the Slave Trade* (1968)

Marcy, P.T., *Eighteenth-century Views of Bristol and Bristolians* (1966)

Mayo, R., *The Huguenots in Bristol* (1985)

Minchinton, W.E., *The Port of Bristol in the Eighteenth Century* (1962)

Morgan, K., *John Wesley in Bristol* (1990)

Mortimer, Russell, *Early Bristol Quakersism* (1967)

Quinn, D.B., *Sebastian Cabot and Bristol Exploration* (1968)

Ralph, Elizabeth, *The Streets of Bristol* (1981)

Ralph, E. and Cobb, P.G., *New Anglican Churches in Nineteenth Century Bristol* (1991)

Sherborne, J.W., *The Port of Bristol in the Middle Ages* (1965)

Sherborne, J.W., *William Canynges, 1402-1474* (1985)

Smith, M.Q., *The Medieval Churches of Bristol* (1970)

Underdown, P.T., *Bristol and Burke* (1961)

Vanes, Jean, *The Port of Bristol in the Sixteenth Century* (1977)

Waite, V., *The Bristol Hotwell* (1960)

Walker, D., *Bristol in the Early Middle Ages* (1971)

Walters, R., *The Establishment of the Bristol Police Force* (1976)

Index

Numbers in bold refer to illustrations.